The Post-Pandemic Nonprofit

12 Disruptive Trends Your Nonprofit Must Master

Jeremy Reis

The Post-Pandemic Nonprofit

ISBN-13 978-0-9760043-6-3

Nonprofit Donor Press

http://postpandemicnonprofit.com

Edited by Sarah Jones.

To my wife Jennica and children, Emily, Evie, Julia, Ellie, Elijah, Josiah, Isaiah, Selah

CONTENTS

INTRODUCTION 1

WHO WE ARE 5

    RENEWING OUR ROOTS 7

    STRATEGIC FOCUS 17

    REDISCOVERING RISK MANAGEMENT 33

    FOSTERING INNOVATION 47

HOW WE OPERATE 57

    REMOTE WORKING 59

    SAFEGUARDING INTERACTIONS 73

    NIMBLE PROGRAM DELIVERY 85

    LOGISTICS & TRAVEL CONSTRAINTS 99

HOW WE GROW 111

    HOW WILL GIVING CHANGE? 113

    IT'S A VIRTUAL WORLD 133

    TRANSPARENCY 149

    ARTIFICIAL INTELLIGENCE 157

WHERE DO WE GO FROM HERE? 167

END NOTES 173

Introduction

Unprecedented times.

How many times have you read, heard, or written these two words during this pandemic? We've used it so many times over the past year that it became cliché; but in many ways, it also became an authentic assessment of our shared experience.

In the nonprofit world, we've had to grow and adapt to this surreal situation and meet challenges we never thought we'd encounter. For example:

- How do we transition nearly all our staff to remote, virtual teams? How do we overcome technology challenges, especially if we have staff on lockdown across the world?

- How do we deliver services to our beneficiaries or clients if the delivery has been primarily face-to-face?

- What will happen to fundraising during a forced economic slowdown? How do we address COVID relief when it is impacting our donors? What does the long-term fundraising landscape look like?

- What will be the impact on our budget?

- How do we prevent the spread of COVID among our staff and the people we serve?

These questions — and hundreds more like them — stretched the capabilities of nonprofit leadership around the globe. What we saw was a remarkable display of teamwork as nonprofits worked through the disruption of normalcy to pivot to new technologies and processes to continue working. We saw teams — from dozens to thousands — shift to working from home, managing both their full-time jobs and the need to care for, and many times educate, their children. We saw teams innovate how to deliver services during a global crisis.

Let me give you an example of a creative way our World Concern team adapted to the crisis in South Sudan. In many areas we work in, it's difficult to reach villages. In South Sudan, we provided evangelists with bicycles so they could travel to remote communities, teach about COVID-19, and deliver much-needed supplies and information. These traveling evangelists took supplies to build hand-washing stations and tell people about how to keep safe.

"We are equipping these evangelists not only with the skills to win souls, but also equipping the church economically, socially, and health-wise," said World Concern South Sudan Country Director Joshua Bundi. "If the church addresses the spiritual needs and fails to address the physical needs of communities, the church fails to address the real man. At this point in time, when the whole world is faced with the challenge of COVID-19, the church must not only pray and encourage its members and communities but must demonstrate to them how to safeguard their families from the virus."

It's stories like this one, multiplied by the millions, that made up the fabric of our lives in 2020.

We learned. We adapted. We suffered. We overcame. We changed.

Don't Just Survive — Thrive

The Washington Post recently cited a survey that a third of nonprofits[i] could close during the pandemic and recession. Unfortunately, many of these nonprofits are responding to human needs — food, shelter, basic needs — and there isn't anyone to fill the gap. Private donors are beginning to cut back while the government isn't able to provide meaningful relief for nonprofits. Richard Malone, President of Y.M.C.A. of Metropolitan Chicago, succinctly explained the problem: "Our twin priorities are service and survival."

The pandemic presented uniquely difficult challenges to nonprofits, but not all the challenges were *caused* by the pandemic. The pandemic brought many of the issues facing nonprofits to light as they could no longer be hidden by healthy fundraising or government grants.

Unfortunately, the nonprofit sector isn't finished with challenging times. The coming months will continue to present stresses to nonprofit organizations. Without sufficient measures, many will be forced to close their doors.

If you do make it through the economic fallout from the pandemic and lockdowns, what is waiting for your organization on the other side? This is what I aim to explore in this book.

Here, you'll find 12 trends impacting the nonprofit sector *and* how these trends have been formed or influenced by the pandemic. Life will be different for nonprofits post-pandemic, so the decisions you make today to set your organization's strategic path will determine whether or not you'll be able to thrive.

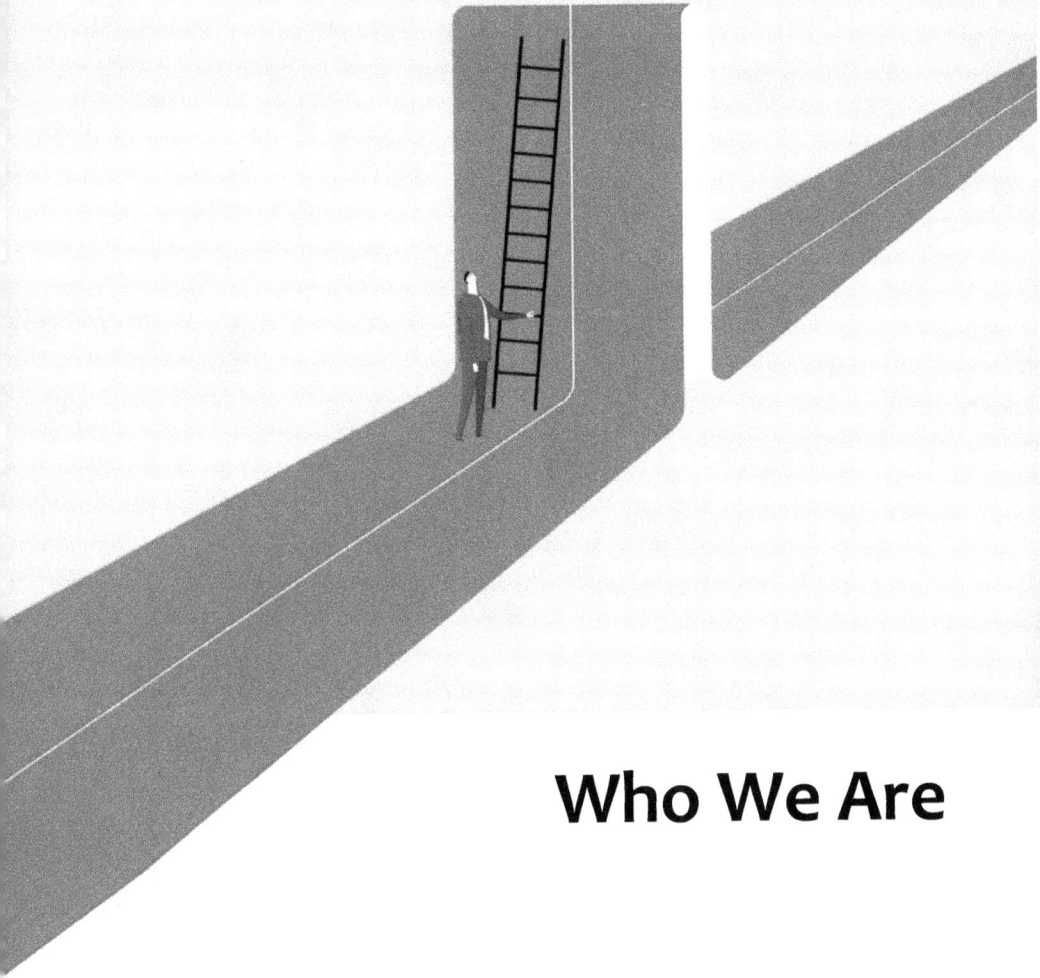

Who We Are

Renewing Our Roots

Traditionally during difficult economic and social times, the social sector has been able to step in and bridge the gap. Unfortunately, during a pandemic, all organizations — both corporate and nonprofit — are equally forced to meet the challenges head on. All organizations are pressured to grow and adapt, but how do you make sure your growth is within the frames of who your organization is?

After the pandemic, nonprofits must operate from a solid foundation. I call this necessity "renewing our roots." Let's explore how to position the organization during lean times to take advantage of the post-pandemic environment.

Mission

Your organization's mission is the guide by which you should operate. The SeaChange organization published a report in 2020 titled *Tough Times Call for Tough Action*.[ii] In it, the organization argued that all your decisions should be guided by the question, "What best advances the long-term mission of the organization?"

In this post-pandemic environment, nonprofit organizations that are focused on accomplishing their mission will be more successful. Why? When the organization's leadership and staff are all aligned with what they need to accomplish, they will be more focused, more productive, and efficient. When everyone is heading in the same direction, it's more likely you'll get there successfully.

Organizations with an unclear mission or staff who don't know or understand the mission have difficulty achieving it.

During boom economic periods, it's easy to let "mission creep" affect your organization. Mission creep is the gradual expansion of a mission beyond its original scope. There are a couple of reasons why mission creep occurs:

We chase funding. Sometimes a grant requires us to operate outside our mission, but we chase the funding, thinking, "It won't hurt to go after funding this one time! Just think of the impact we could make!"

In some cases, a donor offers money to an organization to do work outside its mission. In these situations, it's best to turn down the donation or try to move the donor to give to something within your scope.

A few years ago, I helped a local foster care support organization with a project, and a donor approached them with an idea and a proposed $50,000 grant if they would support several homeless families with similar services. There was considerable debate within the nonprofit organization because 1) the audience and some of the services were outside the organization's mission, and 2) $50,000 could make a considerable budget difference. Whether or not to accept the funding hinged on this question presented by the Executive Director: *If we didn't have this grant proposal, would we do these services?* She also asked, "What happens when this money is spent? Do we fundraise to continue these services, or do we close the program?" The organization opted not to change its mission to support the other group, and the donor gave the money instead to a different organization.

There are times when a donor has a passion for a different type of work, and your organization may find it's better to refer the donor elsewhere rather than take on something outside your organization's mission.

New staff. A new executive director or program staff begins to run programs outside the organization's mission because it aligns with their previous experience. But bottom line: New staff shouldn't drive an organization outside its lane unless the organization is changing its mission.

Jessica, President of an anti-child-trafficking organization based in the Midwest, needed to fill a crucial role in the organization, Program Director. Only 14 months into her tenure, the previous Director resigned after 14 years. It was Jessica's first hire. Tom appeared to be the perfect candidate for the role: eight years' experience at a much larger anti-trafficking organization as a program analyst.

At first, everything in the program area worked well under Tom. But slowly, over the next year, things began to change. Tom added new programs and retired others. It was subtle at first but ultimately started to shift the direction of the organization. Jessica had to create guideposts to help steer the team back into alignment with their mission. Once Tom understood the boundaries, the team once again helped move the organization's programs forward.

New staff can try to mold a nonprofit's mission statement to their own vision and, in so doing, not respect the established boundaries. The executive team and the board of directors' responsibility is to ensure the organization aligns with its mission.

Changing landscape. Another source of mission creep is the changing environment. For example, it would be easy for a nonprofit to perform work outside its mission during the pandemic. Your organization may have seen a need and decided to fulfill it even though doing so is outside the scope of what you usually do. Government restrictions, beneficiary needs, competitor behavior, or funding sources change over time, and it's easy for your organization to slowly move away from the intended mission.

It's time to return to your roots!

First, your mission statement isn't intended to be written on the wall and never referred to again. At Food for the Hungry, we went through a several-month process to replace our traditional "vision, mission, and values" with what we called "The Heartbeat." The Heartbeat of FH introduced a standard set of language that staff referred to often — almost every staff meeting or event features language from The Heartbeat. You could challenge someone based on The Heartbeat. In my role as Senior Director of Marketing, I would challenge new ideas by asking, "How does this fit into The Heartbeat?"

Don't be afraid to ask: How does this new proposal or program fit our mission?

If it doesn't, say "no." Admittedly, it can be hard to do, especially if it means turning down a large grant or potential relationship. But if it doesn't fit your mission, it isn't right for your organization.

It's time to reexamine your programs and whether or not they align with your mission.

Examining Your Programs to Reflect Your Mission

The pandemic and its aftermath have caused many nonprofit organizations to refocus their programmatic work. Much of the refocus is due to financial constraints driving difficult decisions about what the organization can accomplish in a time of austerity. In the past, in an economic boom, it may have been possible for an organization to try things outside its mission — or even things aligned with its mission but outside its core competencies — because it has the cash flow to do it. Now, it's time to reexamine what you do to ensure it reflects your organization's mission and is within your core competencies.

Does your mission statement match what your organization is? There are times when mission creep occurs because external factors cause nonprofits to adapt and change. The organization might retain the same mission statement, but it focuses on a new mission in practice.

The most famous example of a nonprofit changing its mission statement is the March of Dimes. The March of Dimes was founded to "eradicate polio in the U.S." Once the U.S. eradicated polio, the organization had a decision. *Close its doors or change its mission?* The organization evolved into a new mission to help fight for pregnant moms and their babies' health. Today, this is the organization's mission statement:

Prematurity is the #1 killer of babies in the United States. We are working to change that and help more moms have full-term pregnancies and healthy babies. From polio to prematurity the March of Dimes has focused on researching the problems that threaten our children and finding ways to prevent them.

The March of Dimes gives a nod to its history. You may find that your organization has completed its mission or has shifted enough to warrant a mission statement review. It's time to review your mission statement and ensure it matches what your organization is doing today and will be doing for the long-term.

Is the organization working to accomplish your mission? Next, review whether or not you're working toward your mission. Are you still focused on that one potent goal?

For example, this is charity: water's mission statement:

charity: water is a non-profit organization bringing clean and safe drinking water to people in developing countries.

As charity: water reviews each project, it's relatively easy to compare the work it's doing to its mission statement. But what happens if a program is developed that is linked to the mission but isn't directly impacting the mission? For example, what if a member of charity: water's staff in Kenya identifies land rights as a potential barrier to bringing clean and safe drinking water to people in Kenya? If the people don't have land rights, perhaps they won't have the ability to dig a well and provide clean water in a community. With all good intentions, the staff member begins to do work toward land rights. But does that fit charity: water's mission?

Review the projects and programs happening within your organization to ensure they fit within the scope of your organization's mission.

Educate your staff to know your mission and question things that may not fit. A significant challenge nonprofits face is instilling core values into staff. If you randomly pick a staff member somewhere within the organization, will they know your organization's mission statement? Will they be able to even express the mission in the right words? If not, you're not alone. Every nonprofit organization I've worked with has this challenge. The key is to educate your staff and encourage them to ask: *Does this initiative fit the mission?*

Realign your programmatic work to match your mission. If you do identify projects or programs outside the scope of your mission, what will you do? Will you shut down or spin off these programs? Will you expand your mission?

There isn't a right or wrong answer, but your organization will need to consider it. Over the years, Food for the Hungry created different programs and projects that started as innovative ideas but began taking up significant resources. Even if (and likely because) they were successful, the organization would often spin these out to become a separate nonprofit organization focused on that work. For Food for the Hungry, spinning off these organizations was the right decision. For your nonprofit, you may identify a different path to take to address inconsistencies between a program and your organization's mission.

Review your mission statement against your organization's important documents. If you do change your mission statement, your organization may have legal requirements to change it elsewhere. The most common places are on your organization's 990 filing with the IRS and the incorporation documents in your state. Consult your legal counsel to determine if your organization should amend your legal documents to incorporate any changes to your mission statement.

Several years ago, I heard some parenting advice: "I pray I can give my kids a strong enough foundation that when the weight of the world is pressing on them later in life they aren't crushed."

For many nonprofits, this year has been one that has tested foundations. Are you still pointed toward your mission? Is your organization ready to take on the challenges of a post-pandemic world? If you are, the next step is to ensure you are focused on your organization's strategy.

Strategic Focus

"On a very basic and practical level, we are operating in a new norm. It can no longer be business as usual in our shelters, supportive housing programs, group homes, and schools."

—Myung Lee, Volunteers of America – Greater New York

Myung Lee is describing what many nonprofit leaders are experiencing. The new normal is causing organizations to rapidly react as we collectively experience frequent changes. When a challenging decision is needed, and we are in the dark regarding what to do next, it can be hard. It's challenging our leadership skills while stretching our ability to make strategic decisions quickly. It's also forcing us to decide what is essential in our organization.

A fundamental question many nonprofits are asking right now is: *Is our organization doing the right things?*

Examine Strategic Initiatives

Most nonprofits were forced to cut back during the pandemic, and, too often, the cuts were deep and necessary at the time. They may not have been strategic cuts.

Now, executives are going back to those decisions and asking if they made the right choices. Perhaps a current initiative doesn't make long-term strategic sense for the organization, and it's best to eliminate it. Maybe there are new initiatives that make more strategic sense and should be pursued. These are the right decisions to make but require the organization to ensure a strategy is leading the organization.

The global pandemic will have an impact on your strategic plan. Now is the time to review and adjust the plan and prepare for what's to come post-pandemic.

Review your current strategic plan to ensure the organization is on-target and that target makes sense. When I started at Food for the Hungry in 2012, they were two years into the "Envision 2020" strategic plan. Few understood what was in the plan, and we didn't use Envision 2020 to plan each year strategically. Instead, Envision 2020 was more of a predictor of where the organization wanted to go but didn't drive annual strategy plans.

Several years later, we recognized our mistake and created a new three-year strategic plan with annual targets to guide us on a path to accomplish our objectives. The new strategic plan aligned with our mission and values and was adjusted based on events. It wasn't a static plan but rather a breathing document that changed as we changed.

Review your current strategic plan:

- Do the goals make sense?
- Are they aligned with where your organization is right now?
- Are you following the plan?
- Is it used in your annual planning?

- Do your staff and your leadership team know what's in the strategic plan, and do you use it to guide your strategic decisions?

If you answered "no" more often than "yes" to these questions, you may need to develop a new strategic plan.

Change your strategic plan as necessary. The strategic plan isn't meant to be published and be the exact predictor of the path your organization will take over the next few years. You may have an experience like I did while I was at Food for the Hungry and need to change your strategic plan.

CRISTA consists of multiple ministries. We have a strategy for CRISTA and then one for each ministry that's under of the umbrella organization. We recently completed an update of our strategic plans and conducted an annual review and adjustment to the plans. Reviewing and adjusting each year helps your organization stay current with what's happening with internal and external factors forcing the organization to shift.

Distribute your plan to the board of directors and the organization's staff. Get your staff and board's input on the strategic plan. Make a presentation to your leadership team and board of directors and offer them a chance to ask questions and provide feedback.

Do you have a strategic plan? Are you following it? If not, now is an excellent time to develop your plan with the understanding that the next 12-24 months could vary drastically from your plan.

This leads to the next logical question: *How are we doing at "doing the right things"?*

Performance-Focused Management

A key trend to emerge post-COVID will be increased performance management in the nonprofit sector. As organizations will be forced to remain lean for several years, nonprofit leaders will be focused on performance metrics in staff roles throughout the organization.

What does "performance-focused management" mean?

Performance-focused leaders use key performance indicators to manage projects and programs. Nonprofit organizations will decide what to do based on metrics and performance. Programs that aren't meeting the predefined metrics will be revised or eliminated.

The unfortunate reality in the post-pandemic world is that there aren't enough resources to support all the nonprofits operating pre-2020. Building systems and processes to ensure your organization is focused on the programs and services that are most effective will better position your nonprofit to get the funding necessary to survive and thrive.

So how do you manage programs and services through the lens of "performance"?

Develop criteria to review your existing programs or services. The first programs that need to be evaluated for performance are the ones you're already doing. Define the metrics that determine success for your program. For example, if you're managing an after-school reading program, you may define percentage improvement for students when entering the program to the three-month point. You might determine a second metric for progress in reading comprehension scores on standardized tests. Finally, you might measure the number of volunteer hours invested.

After you've defined what you will measure, create goals for each metric that determines your program's success. You can define goals based on your historical data, what similar nonprofits achieve, or averages of similar constituents' data in the region not in your program.

Based on the data you collect, and the goals you want to achieve, how is this program performing? If it's above your goals, great job! Your program is effective. If it's below your goals, it may need adjustments to improve, or you might make the difficult decision that the program isn't effective and needs shut down. Tracking metrics and goals will help you understand how your programs or services perform for the purpose of making educated decisions for a path forward.

Determine the requirements to consider new programs or services. Before you start a new program or service, ask these questions:

- What are we trying to achieve with this program?
- How will we measure effectiveness?
- What is our goal?
- When will we determine program effectiveness?
- What are our predefined options based on the metrics?

Developing the criteria for success before your program starts helps your team be nimbler as data is collected and acted upon.

I consulted with a media organization that was planning to launch a daily devotional email. Before the launch, the organization identified the number of people it wanted to sign up for the product, the target unsubscribe rate, and the target open rate. After launch, the organization met the target number of sign-ups and the target unsubscribe rate, but not the target open rate. Before launch, the organization created several actions to take if the open rate did not meet the target. After changing the subject lines and preview text, the open rate improved to meet the organization's goal. Following the process before launch helped the organization enhance the product and create a better resource for its subscribers.

Conserving Cash

Smart CFOs saw the pending economic crisis and took drastic action to conserve cash flow. Unfortunately, the shutdowns happened so rapidly that many leaders took a hatchet to expenses when a carving knife would have been better. Now is the opportunity to start carving.

One funder I work with had every organization she funds prepare a budget for what happens if the organization's leadership cut 30%, 50%, or 70% of the nonprofit's projected funding. Unfortunately, and depressingly, the Nonprofit Finance Fund's State of Sector report[iii] revealed that less than 25% of nonprofits have more than six months of cash reserves. That's not due to the pandemic — the report has produced the same finding for the past seven years. COVID-19 has likely exacerbated the problem and created a situation where a significant majority of nonprofits have just a few months to no cash reserves.

"It is absolutely true that every nonprofit needs to have adequate cash balances available to support the timing of payroll and other expenses, as well as to pay for unanticipated costs or increases," Kate Barr, Executive Director of the Nonprofits Assistance Fund, explained.

How high should your organization's cash reserves level be? Some organizations use a "months of cash flow" metric to determine this — for example, three months, six months, nine months, or a year of cash flow requirements. A better method of selecting your cash reserves level is this four-step process:

1. **Develop a five-year financial forecast for the organization.** Beyond budget planning, the five-year financial forecast looks at every aspect of the organization and estimates your financial requirements during that period of time.

2. **Identify potential risk over those five years.** Identify and quantify the potential risk during that period of time. What happens if the economy declines? What if you need to replace something significant in your building? What if your organization is sued? What if your systems are hacked, and your donors' credit cards are leaked? Quantify the risk both by the likelihood that it could occur and the potential cost to the organization.

3. **Quantify your risk exposure for each year of your plan.** After you've identified your organization's risk profile, how likely is it for something on the list to happen each year of the five-year plan? Identify the potential cost each year and the probability of the event occurring.

4. **Establish your reserve funding level.** Create your cash reserve requirements by using the list of risks to your organization and probabilities of occurrence to determine how much money you should set aside in reserves. For example, if you have a $5 million budget this year and your risk predictions add up to $2.2 million, you should set your cash

reserve level at $2.2 million and develop a plan to save assets to fund this goal.

Intelligent Cost-Cutting

In May 2020, Oxfam announced it were laying off 1,450 staff and closing operations in 18 countries. The move impacts both Oxfam staff and local partners. The organization was in the middle of a strategic review when the pandemic hit, and financial pressures forced the organization to accelerate its plans.

Regional nonprofits aren't immune to the economic crisis. Cincinnati-based animal rescue All Dogs Come From Heaven came close to shutting down due to giving concerns. Its largest donor, Pet Valu, shut its doors. A for-profit company took back the warehouse space they shared, so All Dogs Come From Heaven had to find new storage space. COVID has dramatically impacted both the operations and the organization's finances, forcing leadership to cut expenses across the board.

In November 2008, the Bridgespan Group surveyed nonprofit leaders, asking them to describe how their organizations were managing during the difficult times. Many of the organizations were seeing funding cuts, but few took cost-cutting measures. Recently, Bridgespan surveyed CFOs and CEOs and found that the "wait and see" attitude from early in the pandemic has evolved to organizations taking forceful actions.

Broad Cost-Cutting Measures

Your organization may find it necessary to institute broad cost-cutting measures to survive the pandemic and economic recession. Many organizations run so thin that the largest budget item — staff — is the one targeted first for cost control measures. However, during this crisis, the demand for services is so high that cutting staff will often equate to a significant decrease in the organization's ability to deliver services. For some organizations, broad cost-cutting measures are going to impact their ability to continue offering services.

So, what are organizations doing on a broad basis to survive the economic downturn?

Negotiated savings. One CFO renegotiated each of the organization's contracts, looking for cost savings from printers to hotel rates. Many of the organization's vendors accepted a lower rate rather than lose the business.

Salary and benefits cuts. Many nonprofits have used salary reductions, furloughs, and reduced or eliminated matching funds for 403(b) or 401(k) retirement plans to retain staff. In San Francisco, Schwab Charitable eliminated bonuses and reduced senior executive salaries to keep as many staff positions as possible.

Strategic Cost-Cutting Measures

"Last fall, we started scenario planning around what our budgets might look like given the economy, paying attention to philanthropic support and how that might change," explained Charles Carter, Senior Vice President and COO of Crittenton Women's Union. "At that point, we decided to be cautious."

In March, CRISTA Ministries readjusted our budget strategy to plan for scenarios where we would be required to cut 30% or 50% of our expenses for the rest of our fiscal year and the next fiscal year. After we developed our FY21 budget, we had to then scenario plan what we would cut in each quarter if revenues declined beyond our planning. Performing this type of planning is difficult but necessary, so that if you're in a similar situation, you'll make strategic decisions based on planning instead of "cutting expenses in the heat of the moment."

Organizations should plan potential adjustments at the front end of the planning process by developing several "what if" scenarios comparable to how we created the 30% and 50% reduction plans — and then further scenario plan for worst-case scenarios for each quarter. Developing these scenarios will help you think through alternative courses of action well before your plans are needed.

Consider this when you're contemplating strategic cost-cutting measures:

Perform targeted cuts. Citizen Schools aligned their budget cuts with a long-term strategic plan. "We have announced a one-week furlough for staff; eliminated cost of living increases while preserving merit compensation;

reduced our organizational bonus structure for achievement of balanced scorecard goals; cut executive salaries by three percent; and set into motion a series of reductions in traditional spending across departments, including consultants and travel," said Emily McCann, COO of Citizen Schools. The organization laid off staff in a targeted manner, starting with a merger of two regional offices in Boston and greater Massachusetts. Emily explained, "These actions were part of the broader strategic reorganization and would have happened in the near future."

Perform line-item adjustments for each month in your calendarized budget. Reviewing each line in your budget and comparing it to your strategic plan will help identify areas to cut. Even if they're minimal, small cuts can quickly add up.

Identify where you can cut to keep as much of your strategic plan in place. For example, if you can cut everyone's salaries by 10% but retain key staff to maintain programs, it may be worth the strategic cut.

Explore Mergers, Restructuring, or Dissolution

If you query GuideStar's nonprofit database, you'll find more than 18,000 water-related charities.[iv] Though some may work in different sectors within clean water, does the world need 18,000 separate water charities, with all their overhead, administrative, and fundraising costs? Perhaps...

What we do know is some nonprofits won't survive the global pandemic. With leading economists predicting a two-to three-year recovery, we may see too many nonprofits fail over the next few years.

What are the alternatives?

Arguably one area that doesn't receive enough attention is promoting mergers and acquisitions in the nonprofit industry. Mergers are somewhat different for nonprofits compared to for-profit corporations. A nonprofit merger doesn't see cash change hands in the form of a "buyout," but instead, one nonprofit's assets are absorbed by the other.

A 2017 study by the Stanford Social Innovation Review found that 88% of the merger cases studied had both the acquiring and acquired organizations stating they were "better off" because of the merger, defined as achieving organizational goals and increasing collective impact.[v]

Why would nonprofits explore a merger?

A nonprofit isn't going to be viable forever. Though often this refers to being financially viable, it isn't limited to that. A nonprofit could be non-viable for many reasons, including retiring leaders with no clear succession plan, the long-term mission is no longer needed, or, the too-often-reason, the nonprofit is or could be insolvent. Instead of restructuring or shutting down the nonprofit, the organization could find another stronger organization to merge with.

Two nonprofits are complementary in how or where they work. There could be water-affiliated nonprofit organizations that work in different areas or follow the same programmatic model, using our example of clean water charities, and a merger makes strategic sense. In fact, there are several examples of water charities merging, including the 2009 merger of H2O Africa and WaterPartners to form water.org and the 2017 merger of Lifetime Wells for Ghana and Wells for Relief, International to create Lifetime Wells International. In the SSIR study of nonprofit mergers, they found in 80% of the cases a previous collaboration existed between the two nonprofits before the merger. This may be one place to start looking if your organization is interested in a merger.

A nonprofit plans to enter a space, and instead of building the infrastructure, the organization seeks a smaller charity to merge with. Boundless Reader, a small, school-based literary nonprofit organization, merged with Working In Schools, a volunteer tutor organization. Working In Schools integrated the Boundless Reader programs into its volunteer programs to become a more effective tutoring organization in Chicago public schools.

A typical merger takes six to 18 months to finish. If your nonprofit organization is exploring this option, it makes sense to have conversations with potential merger partners, especially as situations can rapidly change in the post-pandemic environment.

At the beginning of this chapter, I posed a simple yet challenging question many nonprofits are asking: Is our organization doing the right things?

Keeping the organization aligned with your strategy is a core task of senior leadership. The successful post-pandemic nonprofit develops a strategy, announces it to the board of directors and staff, and ensures it is an active part of managing the organization. Not everything will turn out, and it may carry a risk for the organization when it doesn't. How do we manage that risk and still fulfill our mission? In the next chapter, we'll learn about the risk management trend and what your nonprofit organization will be expected to do in the post-pandemic world.

Rediscovering Risk Management

"COVID-19 taught us valuable lessons," said Rachel, Executive Director of a multi-million-dollar fund. "Few could have seen the events of 2020 coming, but there was a distinct divide between nonprofit organizations who had some risk reduction experience and the ones who didn't."

Many of us were caught without a clear plan on addressing the variety of problems presented, identifying which risks were clearly an issue we needed to handle, or the tools to estimate the risk involved. We aren't experienced risk managers, and our organizations simply weren't prepared. As funders like Rachel discovered, many organizations were not only unprepared for the variety of problems 2020 has presented, but they're unprepared in general for *any* kind of risk.

In 2019, U.S. charities registered $449.64 billion from American individuals, corporations, foundations, and bequests. Total giving was up 4.2% from 2018, and giving by corporations increased the most at 13.4%. According to the Independent Sector's "Health of the U.S. Nonprofit Sector" report, there were 1,729,101 registered nonprofits in 2019, and the nonprofit economic contribution to U.S. GDP was $1.2 trillion.

Yet, as many of those employed by nonprofits can attest, the inner workings of many nonprofits are not always the healthiest. In fact, for too many nonprofits, operating and financial measurements are quite precarious.

The same Independent Sector report found four years ago that a staggering 69% of nonprofits had just three months of cash to cover operating and programming expenses. Only half reached an operating surplus at the end of the fiscal year, and the other half either broke even or reported operating deficits. Again, to those on the inside, these aren't novel findings. While the situation from a budgetary perspective has always been a bit unsteady for many nonprofits, the pandemic and its disastrous effects have industry leaders, donors, and community partners in truly uncharted waters.

The post-pandemic nonprofit must have risk management capability and a defined process to identify, mitigate, and respond to risk.

Funders Recognize the Need for More Risk Planning

Like many nonprofits, funders were caught off-guard with the speed and severity of the pandemic-forced lockdown. To their credit, many began offering flexibility in their grants or shored up nonprofits with additional money to help during a time of cash crunch. One thing funders identified during the pandemic is how few nonprofit organizations have sufficient risk planning and management.

Let's be frank: Most nonprofit organizations are bad at identifying, assessing, and mitigating risks. A 2018 survey found just 27% of nonprofit organizations reported having an enterprise risk management process.[vi]

Very few nonprofit organizations have a dedicated risk management team. Without someone championing risk management, it's difficult for staff to take on a risk management initiative, learn the process, and implement it correctly within an organization.

In 2015, Open Road commissioned a survey of 200 nonprofits and 200 funders. The survey found that one in five projects required contingency funding.[vii] The survey also found that nonprofits were hesitant to discuss what could go wrong with the funder — scared that the funding would be pulled — while funders failed to ask what could go wrong.

In the early 2000s, the William and Flora Hewlett Foundation began holding their annual "Worst Grant Contest." Then-President Paul Brest sought to increase transparency surrounding failure and wanted to create spaces to generate discussion around the foundation's mistakes. In large foundations like Hewlett, poor-performing grants will invariably occur. However, what was noticeable for Brest was when the worst grant was named and subsequently discussed, much of the discussion focused on the things the grantee did wrong, such as financial difficulties and leadership challenges. Over time, Hewlett and other large grant-making institutions began to consider whether all the blame was mistakenly one-sided. *Is there a more significant role foundations can play when granting money? How can funders help secure a future past the current grant for nonprofits they support?*

The "Worst Grant Contest" was later named the "Worst Strategy Contest," as Hewlett concluded that poor funding strategy is a more accurate description of what went wrong (for both the nonprofit and the funder). Today, many large Requests for Proposals (RFPs) incorporate risk management in the application process. Potential funders are asking nonprofits to document and address risks.

First, funders address the financial risk of investing in a nonprofit. Will the organization achieve its impact goals? Can the organization survive after the grant is fulfilled? What does the future look like for the nonprofit organization? 2021 has forced many funders to take a more critical look into these questions than they may have in previous years.

One funder recently told me how she encourages nonprofits to explore mergers with other nonprofits to come out of the pandemic in a stronger position. She believes there's considerable risk in the nonprofit sector, and mergers of similar organizations can be painful in the short-term but increase survival chances in the future.

Second is the reputational risk to the foundation. As history has shown us, granting money to a nonprofit can come back to bite the funder if the nonprofit does not deliver on its proposal or engages in activities that disparage the funder's reputation. Every funder has a different threshold for reputational risk, but, like financial risk, foundations desire risk reduction in a hyper-politicized world.

Foundations have not only incorporated risk management into RFPs, mandating that applicants address these two critical risks, but they are also playing an active role in helping applicants budget for contingency funding. Whereas in the past a contingency budget line item was an arbitrary percentage to cover "miscellaneous costs," foundations now spend a great deal of time examining grantee finances to determine just how large a contingency fund will be needed for a project. Long gone are the days of grantors covering over-budget expenses. Funders are trying to mitigate risks with a more shared, strategic approach to grant-making.

Funders want to invest in organizations that have continuity. After the pandemic, funders will have a renewed focus on risk management and take steps toward requiring nonprofits to have sufficient plans in place.

What does this mean to your nonprofit organization?

If you rely on grants, you will need to develop a risk management capability. It won't be enough to rely on a plan that is inadequate to address risks present in today's environment or one that is several years old.

Understanding Risk Management

As reported in BBB Wise Giving Alliance's "Special Report: COVID-19 and the Charitable Sector," 80% of the surveyed nonprofits expect revenues to be lower than previously expected in 2020. Some estimates suggest 7% of nonprofits will be forced to close due to the pandemic. And while 7% might not sound like a lot, that's a total of 121,037 nonprofits. The average nonprofit employs approximately six to 10 individuals, so anywhere from 726,222 to 1,210,370 people face potential unemployment. This isn't to mention the millions of direct recipients of help from these agencies who will undoubtedly suffer due to their closures.

the Federation Employment Guidance Services (FEGS), a prominent New York-based nonprofit federation, closed its doors for good in 2015. With a $250 million budget, FEGS was a massive player in the city, serving roughly 120,000 individuals annually and employing nearly 2,000 people. The FEGS bankruptcy hit the sector like a ton of bricks. If a behemoth like FEGS could fail, no nonprofit was safe.

Post-bankruptcy, the FEGS case was studied extensively. There were many underlying reasons for its failure. Still, perhaps the most relevant was its neglect in identifying risks (internally and externally) that the institution faced and developing a corresponding plan to mitigate them. On the structural side, nonprofits face a series of risks that have only been exacerbated by the pandemic. Many nonprofits receive the bulk of their funding via restricted grants or government funding. The arrival of both, but the latter in particular, is subject to unpredictable delays. This demands that nonprofits have enough cash on hand to execute and deliver what the grant or funding is earmarked to cover before the money arrives in most circumstances.

A majority of nonprofits also provide labor-intensive, face-to-face services. Like the education sector, the cost of providing these services increases faster than inflation. Moreover, these services do not become more productive with the adoption of new technology. As such, it is difficult to trim costs at the margin by reducing the workforce. While machine learning and artificial intelligence add tremendous value to the sector, they will not have the same cost-saving effect as banking, insurance, manufacturing, or healthcare.

Employing individuals with a passion for serving and a willingness to take lower pay has often been challenging for nonprofits. There is a sizeable pool of talented people willing to earn less in exchange for being part of a philanthropic organization, but it's challenging retaining them and providing career development. Ultimately, most nonprofits operate in highly dynamic environments. Political priorities, the pervading fashionable causes of the moment, and a host of other ever-changing factors can make it difficult for some nonprofits to remain relevant.

The Global Fund's mission is to fight AIDS, tuberculosis, and malaria in countries with the greatest need. The Fund has identified risk in doing this type of work, and managing the risk improves the probability of a particular project's success. One of the critical priorities for the Fund is to help organizations manage risks. To this end, it provides tools for nonprofits it works with to teach risk management down to the in-community project implementers.

As funders expect nonprofits to identify and manage risk, you'll find them consolidating grants to organizations that display this skill set. More importantly, risk management can improve an organization's longevity by identifying potential risk, mitigating the exposure as much as possible before it happens, and developing a plan to address risk you cannot mitigate if it happens.

Remember: it's not possible to eliminate all risk. A successful risk management strategy is one tailored to the specific needs of your organization.

Why is risk management critical? It should be clear at this point that running a nonprofit, no matter the size, without a risk management plan is a recipe for disaster. Aside from the structural issues, at a more granular level all nonprofits face risks in their corporate structure, governing documents, policies and policy manuals, tax-exempt status (and corresponding compliance), financial condition, insurance coverage, personnel, public relations, physical safety, and leadership succession, among many other areas. Risks are identifiable, while uncertainties are issues that pop up unexpectedly. However, uncertainties can turn into risks, and the point of a risk management plan is to put a system in place that can control and provide a roadmap for how to address the things you can mitigate as an institution.

For many nonprofit leaders and trustees, this isn't ground-breaking news. Nonprofit leaders know risks exist, but because of a lack of time, resources, or qualified risk management staff, a proper risk management plan isn't developed, and many are caught unprepared when disaster strikes. It's vital for your organization to create an appropriate risk management plan — starting now.

When should we start implementing a risk management plan? Any business, nonprofits included, begins taking on risks the second it is operational. Following this logic, a risk management plan should be one of the first things trustees or founders focus on, right? When nonprofits find themselves in the startup phase, the focus is on viability. The project needs to get off the ground, attract funding, and deliver results to be viable. Suppose trustees and founders divert too much of their attention to risk mitigation and management plans. In that case, the all-too-important ideation and creativity needed for the launch will be compromised.

Now, this isn't to say there should be no talk of risk management to begin. An insurance policy will cover most of what could go wrong and is an appropriate first step before a full-fledged plan. Yet once a nonprofit reaches the end of that start-up phase, several things will occur. First, retaining and continuing to attract high-quality donors will be a priority, requiring regular audits. Second, the board of directors will move from being a working board to a governance board and will formalize policies and procedures.

It is at this point that a risk management plan is vital for five fundamental reasons. First, a nonprofit can only understand its priorities if its leaders also understand their risks as an organization. Building a risk management plan helps the organization identify which programs and services have the highest risk and should be given a reduced priority to reflect the associated risk.

Second, short- and long-term planning is a priority, led by the organization's strategic plan. A good strategic plan is not complete without the Strengths, Weaknesses, Opportunities, and Threats (SWOT) analysis. Identifying the risks that coincide with weaknesses and threats is a vital part of the risk management plan.

Third, donors who begin to become multi-year supporters are interested in the effective performance of the nonprofit. No donor is happy to discover their gift went to an organization that closed shop because it couldn't mitigate risks. A risk management plan helps nonprofits understand the challenges that could negatively affect the solvency of the institution.

Fourth, one goal of all organizations is to be sustainable. In the early years, nonprofits focus on the services they provide to their users or clients. In future years, the nonprofit needs to pivot to ensure stability, sustainable funding, and efficient programs and services. The risk management plan helps create stability for the nonprofit by defining mitigations for possible risks.

And finally, we return to insurance. As the organization initially implemented an insurance policy to cover unexpected issues, insurance shifts risks to a third party. It does not, and cannot, provide early warnings or response mechanisms for those threats that emerge along the way. The only strategy that can do this is a risk management plan.

How do we identify risk? Most nonprofits are made up of three functional areas: internal, external, and overarching. The internal area is typically comprised of Operations, IT, and Finance, among others. External could be Sales, Development, and Marketing, while overarching is Governance and Compliance.

An operational risk management plan first requires a risk inventory. This is where the nonprofit surveys the threats and opportunities across these three functional areas. A well-crafted risk inventory involves a range of folks — best practice suggests a senior staff member, one or more employees at an entry or middle-management level, and a relevant stakeholder (a donor or member of a partner agency). In some circumstances, you may want to include a board member who has relevant experience. The inclusion of the entry or middle-level employee helps the senior staff member avoid tunnel vision or groupthink. The donor or outside partner tends to provide insight that an insider might not consider.

After the risks have been identified, it is time to rank and identify owners. Not all risks are the same. Some are understandably much more important than others, so a simple ranking process (1 to 4) is imperative. It's also crucial to assign ownership for each risk to ensure there is a central decision-maker.

For each risk identified, the responsible staff member should identify:

1. Risk impact (low, medium, high)
2. Risk likelihood (low, medium, high)
3. Risk owner (Who is responsible for managing this risk?)
4. Internal teams impacted

Without an owner, a risk remains a threat without a pre-defined response. Most owners are departments and not individual people. However, if the nonprofit is small, and the Marketing team is one person handling marketing and communications duties, any risk aligned with that department will invariably be the responsibility of that person. If this is the case, assigning a senior leader to monitor those risks associated with Marketing, in this instance, is recommended. A resulting "risk register" will house the identified risks, their level of importance, and their owners. This register then becomes a regular agenda item in staff meetings moving forward.

Lastly, it is imperative to communicate that a risk management process can take time, especially when achieving widespread adoption and acceptance. Timelines and goals need to be set with milestones to measure progress. While the risks and their respective owners will be addressed weekly, training the organization's staff and board of directors on how to think about mitigating risks will take time.

What is risk mitigation? Risk mitigation is the process you use to reduce the chance a risk may happen, decrease the potential impact from the risk, shield the organization from the risk, prepare for what happens if a risk occurs, or compensate for potential risk.

For example, your organization has a risk that an employee will become the victim of a phishing scheme and give his or her password to a nefarious party. This could provide a bad actor access to sensitive systems. Risk mitigation could include:

- Limiting user access to necessary systems only.
- Firewalls to prevent external connections from reaching internal systems.
- Training for staff to reduce the chance of falling for a phishing scheme.
- Frequently forced password changes.
- Security intrusion systems scanning for abnormal behavior.
- Limiting data downloads for user accounts to the average amount needed to eliminate large-scale data access.
- Purchasing insurance against data loss.

These are just seven of the many potential actions you could take to mitigate the risk of an employee divulging a password to a bad actor. Some of these are system changes, others are preventative (like training), while some are helping compensate for potential loss (like the insurance). Each element protects the organization from a specific part of the risk, and, as a whole, they help reduce risk exposure for the organization.

For each of the risks identified in the previous step, pinpoint potential mitigation strategies and how they will affect both risk impact and risk likelihood. For example, you may identify a risk that your donor's credit card information could be compromised in your donation management system with a medium-risk likelihood and a high-risk impact. If you use a hosted credit card solution that doesn't store credit card information on your systems, you could reduce your risk likelihood and impact to low.

Any significant disruption to the U.S. and the world economy will likely put your nonprofit in a difficult position. It could introduce new, unforeseen risks that threaten your existence. A sound risk management plan will consider disruptive events and create the tools and procedures to address them before a shock occurs. When you sufficiently address risk, it encourages the opportunity to innovate.

Fostering Innovation

Many nonprofits are implementing stop-gap measures designed to keep their organizations viable and their staff employed. What lies ahead is a world of uncertainty where the beneficiaries increasingly need a given organization's services.

During this pandemic crisis, the novel solutions nonprofits have created are resourceful and creative. Organizations shifted operations online, developed ways to deliver services in a no-contact world, and pivoted to provide complementary services to people with the greatest need. Organizations rapidly shifted their operations and pursued swift innovation when just keeping the lights on was a challenge.

Innovation is one of the most undervalued aspects of nonprofit organizations. They are often driven to innovate with a lack of resources and funding. Without enough people to get something accomplished, nonprofits develop innovative solutions. For example, when institutions wouldn't create financial solutions for people in developing nations, nonprofits came up with the framework for community savings groups. Community savings groups served as a microbank in many communities, providing loans and savings accounts to serve the most vulnerable. Where a bank had no way to fund a woman who desired to start her own sewing business, the community savings group would affordably invest, enabling a new entrepreneur to provide for her family and, hopefully, provide a tidy profit for other community members.

Innovation isn't something you can add to someone's job description and tell them to achieve it. The most innovative organizations build it into their culture and allow staff the freedom to develop and test new ideas. Even if your organization hasn't been innovative in the past, you can transform the culture to encourage novel thinking.

Dr. Ashwin Vasan, President and CEO of Fountain House, found this out at the beginning of the pandemic. "The disruption to our business model forced us to pivot in several ways," he explained. "We had to move quickly, start from scratch, and ask a set of questions about what our impact can look like moving forward — questions that we've never thought about before."

Fountain House offers services to help those living with mental illness to live, work, and learn. Dr. Vasan explains that Fountain House is a "very analog" organization that was forced to develop ways to offer services in no-contact situations. In a few weeks' time, the organization used hosted software solutions for video conferencing and digital meetings with program participants. This new Virtual Clubhouse enabled Fountain House to reach more people and to connect better with young participants who are more digital-savvy.

As your organization looks for how it can innovate past the pandemic and into the future, you can start by:

Identifying Your Core Competencies

The first step to creating an innovation-oriented culture is to identify the core competencies for your organization. What are you good at? How did you get good at those things? When you identify your strengths, it helps shape how you can deliver those services differently in the future. After you identify your core competencies, break them down into these basics: what, who, why, how, and where.

For example, imagine a nonprofit organization that connects volunteer tutors to schools with students experiencing learning challenges. The organization might identify these core competencies:

1. Reading programs
2. Math instruction
3. Student mentoring

Break each one down into the elements. Let's do this with the first core competency:

What: Reading instruction to help bring students up to their grade level in reading comprehension.

Who: Volunteers from the local community.

Why: Students in the local school who are one or more grade levels behind in reading comprehension.

How: Volunteers use pre-assigned books to help students in the after-school program.

Where: At the local school.

After you've identified each element of your core competencies, you're ready for the next task: to examine the fundamental assumptions about your work.

Examining Fundamental Assumptions About Your Work

A method for fostering innovation is to examine the fundamental assumptions about how you work. Many organizations fall into the we've-always-done-it-this-way trap, assuming the way it has been done is the most efficient and effective method. In reality, it's difficult to break from tradition. *What if a new way of doing things fails? We know this method works; why try something new? Is it a wise investment of donor dollars to try something new when we have something that's proven effective?* These are valid questions, but they keep your organization from the critical need to continue improving.

Becoming an innovative organization has many benefits. When presented with crises, the organization develops solutions that attract attention and funding, and it encourages freedom for employees to try new things. When employees feel this kind of freedom, they are more likely to stay with the nonprofit.

A framework we've found useful in examining fundamental assumptions about your work contains these four questions:

1. What are you doing?
2. How are you doing it?
3. Where are you working?
4. Why are you doing it this way?

We all have fundamental assumptions about our work processes. Some come from experience, others from assuming that someone before us has developed this into a finely tuned process. When you start questioning processes, programs, and services, you may find an opportunity for improvement. Be prepared to write down the answers to these questions. When you are forced to write down the answers, you'll identify opportunities for improvement. Let's explore each question.

What are you doing? Describe what you are trying to accomplish. Write down a description of your program, process, or product. When you describe what you are doing, it helps you understand the purpose and identify what you could accomplish.

The JED Foundation promotes mental health and works to prevent suicide among teens and young adults. During the COVID crisis, JED brought together students, parents, mental health experts, and teachers to identify how the COVID crisis affects youth. JED leaders desired to identify gaps in their programmatic offerings and make sure they were adequately addressing the mental fallout from the current crisis. They found several gaps, one of them in helping the Asian-American youth population. They identified that many of these young adults were facing bullying. The organization expanded its programs to help Asian-American youth experiencing xenophobia. The JED Foundation experience shows that by questioning what they were doing, they identified gaps in the communities they could serve.

How are you doing it? Document your process to understand what you are doing. When you start writing down a process, you might immediately discover tweaks that will improve your process. You will also identify critical spots to move beyond incremental improvement and innovate your work.

At one organization I worked for, we had a staff member retire after many decades. As we documented the processes she followed, we found several spots for improvement. For example, in one step, she had 27 copies of what we were producing created and stored. When we asked, "Why 27?" she explained that it was what she had always done. We had storage closets full of boxes of these materials that we rarely reviewed. We consulted with our legal team and found we only needed to retain a single copy, but we kept a few in storage and disposed of the rest. As we reviewed how we were doing things, we found several points for process improvement that saved the new staff member who replaced her hours each week.

Where are you working? List the geographic places in which you are working. Is there an opportunity to do this same program somewhere else? If you move it, what will need to change? How would the program be different?

The geographic or physical location you're working in matters to your program or process. For example, suppose you're creating a community savings group program in certain parts of the world. In that case, you might incorporate cell phones into the procedure, while pen and paper are the only options in other parts of the world. The physical location where you're delivering a service also matters. Developing an after-school reading program that meets in a school verses a library verses the local YMCA all have different logistical challenges to address.

In South Sudan, World Concern helps evangelists plant churches. One of the difficulties the organization encountered was transportation to some of the areas it wanted to reach. There weren't roads to many of these remote communities. So we came up with a solution: to purchase off-road bicycles for the evangelists to reach these communities. Such a move expanded the geographic reach of the program.

Why are you doing it this way? This may be the most challenging question to answer. You might have to dig into some history to understand why a process is designed the way it is. It's possible you find no one knows why. When you start digging into the "why" for each step in a process, you might find ample opportunities to improve your process or innovate something new.

Several years ago, I worked for a nonprofit, and the IT development team decided we were a specific type of web development shop based on the longest-serving employee and the technology he used. We began an improvement process and challenged the assumption that we were tied to a specific technology because of this single staff member. It wasn't an easy discussion — and took several months to resolve. In the end, we made a shift in technology and created several cutting-edge web solutions on a different platform. We were willing to address why we were doing something a specific way, and the changes we made resulted in significant improvements in our digital platforms.

Discussing Solutions with Those Closest to the People

You cannot build a solution in a vacuum. Often, the people who know what works best are closest to the nonprofit organization's beneficiaries. When you engage your frontline staff and volunteers, you may find innovative ideas you couldn't have discovered among your office staff.

Capture innovative ideas within your organization. When Mike Meyers was the CEO at Food for the Hungry, he began an initiative to capture and encourage innovative ideas. He knew the organization couldn't rest on the past successes but needed to identify innovative ideas and implement them. The challenge — with over 3,000 global employees — was with how the ideas are identified, documented, tested, and deployed to other organization regions. Mike created cross-functional teams to help encourage innovation and to look at problems in different ways.

Food for the Hungry's structure had a leader over all international operations, a regional director, country directors, and regional staff within each country. Country directors were encouraged to try new things. A history of fostering an innovative culture led to one of the first microfinance banks, innovations in savings groups in Africa, new ways to quickly grow aquatic food for chickens in the Dominican Republic, and effective church partnerships in the Philippines.

You can implement an innovation-friendly culture in your nonprofit by encouraging staff to try new ideas. Model innovation at the top. Organizations where failures are punished instead of seen as learning opportunities crush creativity from blossoming. As a nonprofit leader, you must make sure your leadership team encourages intelligent risk-taking and imagination. One method to promote an innovative culture is to create testing teams to discover and test new ideas rapidly.

Create rapid testing teams for new ideas.

Literacy organization Springboard Collaborative accelerated efforts to teach low-income students to read in light of the COVID pandemic's lockdowns. Since meeting with students in-person wasn't feasible, the organization put together innovation teams of Springboard leaders, parents, and teachers to participate in sprints to create remote learning experiences for children. Instead of creating focus groups, these teams had parents and teachers use prototypes and offer real-time feedback on what worked — and what didn't.

"The only way to prevent COVID-19 from deepening inequality for an entire generation of children is to learn with the most vulnerable," said Alejandro Gibes de Gac, Founder and CEO of Springboard Collaborative.

Some organizations attempt to innovate from the top-down, yet few organizations can achieve real innovation through an authoritarian model. Instead, organizations that allow organic innovation and create cross-functional testing teams to identify which ideas hold promise will succeed in the post-pandemic world.

"COVID is laying bare a level of urgency and opportunity. This is a moment for us to lead and to disrupt what has stood in the way of the change we've wanted — and to accelerate what's possible."
—Mora Segal, Chief Executive of Achievement Network

It may be a challenge for an organization facing funding and operational challenges to re-imagine itself and innovate new solutions to achieve its goals. But as many nonprofit organizations have proven over the years, innovation will be a foundation that the next set of thriving nonprofits will build on.

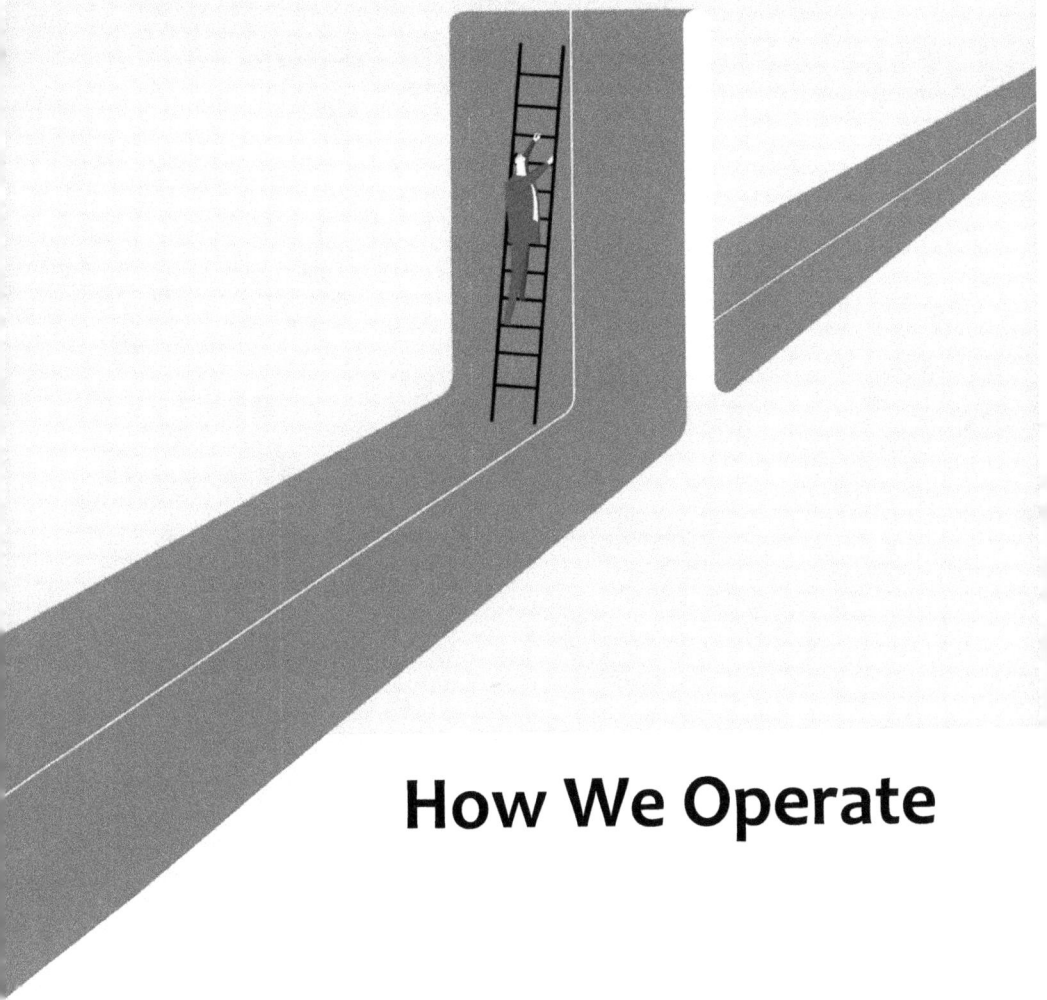

How We Operate

Remote Working

Twenty-year-old Portland-based health services nonprofit OCHIN is selling its 40,200 square feet headquarters and transitioning all staff — including the 272 staff at its headquarters — to virtual work.

"Like many organizations, we shifted to a remote workforce in order to keep our staff and community safe throughout the pandemic," said OCHIN CEO Abby Sears. "What we've learned since then is a fully virtual model suits us well. It allows us to offer more flexibility for our staff and more nimble, regional support for our members across multiple time zones. The future of both work and healthcare is virtual — this shift will help ensure that OCHIN stays on the forefront of that transformation as we grow."

Like OCHIN, Lifeway is looking to sell or lease its three-year-old 279,770-square-feet headquarters in downtown Nashville. The Christian resource retailer nonprofit is looking to reduce its office footprint in a $25 million cost-savings plan. The organization was only using about 60% of the space daily pre-COVID as it offered a "robust work-from-anywhere" plan with its staff.

Many other nonprofit organizations are ending leases and selling office buildings as they find staff productive in work-from-home arrangements. There are challenges to maintaining a virtual team, but remote working is a trend nonprofits must address during and after the pandemic.

Nonprofits Will Need to Offer Flexible Workweeks

Working from home is enjoying broad support in the for-profit sector, with more than half (55%) of corporate executives expecting to support flexible workweeks permanently.[viii] Office employees desire flexibility above all, with 83% desiring to work from home at least one day per week.

A recent survey by Forbes found that 69% of nonprofits have accommodated work from home for all staff during the pandemic. An equal percentage is planning on offering remote work after the pandemic passes.[ix] Like their nonprofit counterparts, 70% of for-profit firms required staff to work from home during the worst of COVID-19.

This isn't to say working from the office is over. Though some organizations are deciding to end office leases or sell their buildings during the crisis, both staff and executives benefit from working together in person. Employers desire to see high productivity levels combined with collaboration and community. At the same time, employees want flexible work options to alleviate the pressure of being "always on" but still desire connection and community with coworkers.

Nonprofits will need to offer flexible work options to retain the best staff. If they refuse, they're at risk of losing staff to other nonprofits or to the for-profit sector that will offer flexibility among their benefits.

Many nonprofit executives will want to return to the office for collaboration and keep an eye on their teams. Staff will desire continued flexibility with the option to meet together for collaboration and community.

How will you balance these desires?

Nonprofit executives must recognize that remote work doesn't result in less productivity, evidenced by the productivity levels accomplished in 2020. Where management structures for what was perceived as temporary remote work were hastily added initially, the last several months have allowed for an improved definition of working remotely. This may not be enough; for long-term work flexibility, building a robust management capability is required to maximize productivity and work happiness for staff. Some managers may have difficulty adjusting to managing remote employees and need expanded training and tools to be influential leaders. Staff will be happier, and managers will get more accomplished with a method for performing work in a flexible environment. It comes down to providing people with what they need to be productive.

For some nonprofit leaders, a permanent flexible work policy is a bridge too far. How do you overcome the challenge of a leader who dislikes remote work? First, document how productive staff members were during the throes of the pandemic. Second, develop a strong work-from-home policy. You must understand that different leaders have different worldviews and may have had a bad experience in the past with an employee who took advantage of work-from-home arrangements. Writing a policy creates a frame for the executive to precisely understand what "work from home" means in your specific nonprofit context.

Pre-pandemic, Food for the Hungry offered staff Tuesday or Thursday as a remote day. Defining the particular days available and creating expectations for staff helps managers lead their teams well.

Finally, explain how other organizations are offering flexible work options. Not offering this benefit may result in staff leaving for greater flexibility. Nonprofit organizations often trail for-profit businesses in an economic recovery, and when employment rates recover, nonprofit staff could leave for more money and flexibility. Offering a cash flow-friendly benefit like flexible work schedules may keep your best employees with your organization.

All of this isn't meant to be a one-size-fits-all approach. Certain work functions need a secure office space. For example, processing checks from donors can be challenging in a remote work environment and be a step too far for many organizations. For these types of roles, organizations will need to determine if the position must be in an office or if an alternative can be found. For example, many organizations use a vendor to process incoming donations via checks and credit card information securely.

What are the challenges nonprofit organizations will need to overcome to offer flexible workweeks for staff? We've identified six.

Better technology and equipment. At the beginning of lockdowns, many organizations rushed to migrate staff members toward working at home, often with the equipment they had from the office. For workers with robust technology at home, the transition may have been easier to make than for those with fewer devices. For example, workers who need scanners and printers to function may have been sent home without those devices, and they had to be creative in finding alternate solutions.

Likewise, collaboration tools became a challenge as organizations quickly deployed programs such as Microsoft Teams, Slack, or Zoom. To their credit, the companies behind those products did an excellent job scaling up to meet corporate, education, and nonprofit clients' demands. Organizations that did not implement these types of collaborative tools may have felt the pain as their staff felt alone and were challenged to continue working in a team atmosphere. Nonprofits without information technology staff on the payroll were most challenged during this time, deploying solutions ad hoc without the necessary support mechanisms in place.

Nonprofit organizations will need to evaluate corporate tools to increase productivity, communication, and collaboration. They will need to ensure the tools implemented are the right ones for the organization and that the structure they were implemented with during the pandemic is suitable for the long-term. For example, during the pandemic, your organization may have rushed to set up the teams and channels in a collaboration tool that doesn't work efficiently for your staff's day-to-day. Fix these problems quickly so it doesn't grow out of control.

Staff may also require additional hardware to perform their jobs. From security tools such as firewalls to printers or scanners, provide your staff with the necessary means to accomplish their jobs. Organizations will need to judiciously choose how to deploy these assets to keep costs under control and ensure the right tools land with the right workers.

Greater flexibility in work hours. The traditional eight-hour work block in an office may not be the most effective for the at-home worker. For example, one software developer at a regional nonprofit does his most productive work with a four-hour block in the middle of the night and a four-hour block in the afternoon. Few other staff may prefer this schedule, but he finds it refreshing to break up his workday. He can attend meetings and interact with staff in the afternoon and spend a concentrated period of time in software code where he doesn't require interaction with other staff.

Other jobs may require more collaboration driving the need for schedules aligned with their teams. Many employees found their workday is more productive when broken up by a walk around the block or eating meals at non-traditional times. Nonprofit executives should be flexible with work schedules to increase effectiveness from staff. We recommend allowing staff to determine work hours and create meetings and interaction times around their schedule.

Clear expectations for availability and response time. One concern some managers had of remote staff is ensuring availability and response time. *What happens if I have a question that I need an immediate answer for? What if my staff member is off at a doctor's appointment or changing the oil in his car?* For most, the pandemic proved these fears unfounded. In other situations, a quick correction of the employee solved the problem. Regardless, setting clear expectations for availability and response time during typical working hours establishes trust that employees can communicate when required.

Good policies don't replace good leadership. Train your executive team to manage your remote staff effectively and use policies to enforce the unordinary cases where a staff member is ineffective in their work.

Increased check-ins and open communication. Staff members crave communication opportunities with leadership. With an abrupt change to working alone at home, the need for interaction increased. Many staff and leaders struggled with this during the pandemic. I had several people reach out and ask how to improve communication and build a team during a time when people couldn't interact in person. Many of these teams had high interaction with frequent meetings and social time together over the coffee pot or water cooler. As a leader, you must develop ways to increase your check-ins with staff and continue to let them know you're open to communication. Develop a pattern of checking your staff's mental well-being without talking about KPIs or metrics. Ask people, "How are you doing?" and don't accept "Fine..." as an answer. At CRISTA, our Chief Development Officer Mike Meyers began purposefully scheduling one-on-one meetings with staff members who weren't his direct reports, as he found when he discussed his open-door communication policy, few (or none) would take him up on his offer to chat. So, he began intentionally scheduling meetings with people.

"A consistent theme we've seen in exit interviews of staff is they don't feel like they can communicate with the executive team. For the first half of the one-on-one, I just ask about people's families and how things are going for them," Mike explained. "For the last half, I ask what we can do better to help support them."

Many staff members need a sense of community to be productive and happy. These folks often socialized together outside of work pre-pandemic, but being under a stay-at-home order was creating a tremendous amount of stress. One leader I know is scheduling a weekly social hour for his team at 5 p.m. on Thursdays. It's optional, but he's found it has helped staff open up about the challenges of working from home during this time — they feel heard, appreciated, and part of the community again.

Increased visibility into results. Holly, one major donor representative, shared how challenging it is to understand whether she was meeting her goals: "In previous years, we had a whiteboard that was updated with fundraising results each day during the year-end fundraising push. It's been difficult identifying how we do this virtually, so I'm not sure how we're doing meeting our fundraising goals."

At CRISTA, we've solved this problem with a weekly video call check-in to share results and an email sent each Friday communicating the updated fundraising totals to all Resource Advancement staff. When your staff is working remotely, you have to think about sharing information and keeping the team updated deliberately. When you don't, they'll begin to suspect there is trouble, and that can lead to unproductiveness, or worse, your best staff leaving.

Improved virtual coaching tool set. Many managers were unprepared to lead staff remotely when stay-at-home orders began around the world. It requires a different skill set to lead a team of remote staff, especially one where the staff has never been managed remotely, and the leader doesn't have experience with it either. Successful organizations are implementing training programs and providing tools to help managers and executives learn how to coach people remotely. The pandemic also increased the perceived "busy-ness" of staff and their leaders, especially ones who now had to deal with children learning from home. Unfortunately, the increased time commitments resulted in some leaders failing to invest in learning new techniques to coach staff remotely.

JVS Human Services, a Michigan-based nonprofit in Southfield, began offering a four-session "Work From Home

Success Group" on Zoom. "Many of us had a significant change in employment starting about eight months ago," said Jason Charnas, JVS Director of Business and Career Services. "This is an opportunity to bring a group of people together that want to talk about how we can do this better."

Learning to manage and coach a team remotely gives a leader a new skill set that is vital as the remote work trend continues to accelerate.

Rethinking Office Space

One sizeable multinational nonprofit based in New York City has vacated its expensive office space and moved all its staff to remote work. After the transition, many workers decided to move out of the city and are now based all over the country. The organization is considering creating smaller office hubs nationwide to maintain collaboration with flexibility for staff to work from anywhere. The move will reduce overall office space expense while creating flexibility for existing staff and expanding the ability to hire talent outside the NYC area.

The pandemic offers nonprofit executives flexibility to consider alternative options for office space. Specifically, you should consider these questions:

1. Does your nonprofit have a specific reason for the office space where you're located now?

2. What management structures do you need in place if you were to consider new office locations or a reduction in square footage?
3. Which benefits do you gain by expanding your ability to hire anywhere? What are the negatives?
4. How can we use coworking spaces with short-term leases for staff who need an office to work from?

Before the pandemic, many leaders considered office space a fixed expense, but as the forced office shutdowns began to wear on, they were considering alternative plans for office leases. But do you need to be in the geographic location you're in now? If your nonprofit is a local service organization, maintaining a physical office may be a requirement; but what if your organization is an international charity with no local programmatic work? Your geographic location may be there because of history or tradition, but as the world reorders itself and emerges from COVID, are you required to work in that city? If you're in an expensive city such as San Diego, New York City, or Boston, it may make sense to relocate to a lower-cost area or move to flexible work environments.

If you decide to reduce or eliminate a central office, what management structures do you need to ensure productivity? How will you accomplish your goals with reduced in-person contact? How will you ensure collaboration and a sense of community continue? These are crucial questions to answer before rethinking your physical office situation.

Jessica, the Executive Director of an international children's charity, explained her leadership team's challenging discussions. "There are no simple answers to the question of eliminating the headquarters," Jessica said. "Though we work outside of the U.S., one of our core values was to have our presence known in Minneapolis. Eliminating the office and allowing staff to work from anywhere could dilute our efforts."

As Jessica and her team worked through the variables of reducing the office footprint, they concluded the organization should maintain a space that would be drastically reduced in size. "An essential part of our decision-making process was to involve staff in the decision. We surveyed all staff and then had each manager speak one-on-one with individual staff to determine their preferences. A majority of staff wanted to work from home most of the time — even after COVID — but have opportunities to come together when necessary. We still have a lot of work to do for a future that looks vastly different than the past few decades at our organization."

Like Jessica and her team, your nonprofit's leadership will need to consider many variables in rethinking how you will move forward with your office space.

Redesigning Workspaces to Offer More Collaboration

The 200-year-old social services organization Sheltering Arms in New York City is selling part of its real estate portfolio as service offerings change and for increased collaboration among staff.

"They needed more space to allow for continued growth, and they wanted an inclusive and collaborative workspace," Commercial Real Estate Broker Stephen Powers said. "No one is going to have a dedicated office in the new space. It's really democratic. Elizabeth, the CEO, will have a workstation like everyone else."

As Lifeway reduces its office space, the organization plans to keep a communal office and meeting area. The flexible office space won't have assigned desks or offices, which will allow teams to collaborate when they are there in person. Additionally, the flexible meeting space will allow larger groups to meet together. One of the things we cannot do during the pandemic is offer collaborative spaces for teams to work closely together — but post-pandemic, there will be a high demand for spaces designed for this.

Like Sheltering Arms and Lifeway, your organization may find a dramatic redesign of space is required if you shift to a flexible work policy. How do you identify and predict what your workspace requirements will be post-pandemic?

First, develop a plan for your work arrangements after the pandemic. Will you let staff pursue flexible work plans? Will you allow and even encourage people to work from home? Perform a needs assessment and identify which positions will be permitted to work from home. Survey your staff and determine who may choose to work from home in the future.

Second, assess what kind of office needs you will have after the pandemic. Do you need a quiet space for staff to work alone? Will you need collaborative space for teams to meet together? Will an open office format work, or do you need separate meeting rooms? Can you create a modular workspace that can be shifted for different types of needs? This step requires your team to toss the past patterns and think about different team needs as work arrangements in the future evolve.

Finally, how will you provide office space for positions that are required to be in the office? Some positions work in sensitive areas or require a set space to achieve their goals. How will you support these needs? What will your policy be for staff who choose to work full-time in the office? Answer these questions to ensure you cover all types of conditions.

"COVID has changed a lot of things," said OCHIN CEO Abby Sears. Remote working and office space will be under significant pressure to change in the post-pandemic business environment. Flexible work arrangements are a trend that will continue and will create new opportunities for teams to thrive. A side benefit for organizations is this trend may offer considerable expense savings as office space is downsized or eliminated.

Safeguarding Interactions

"The COVID-19 health crisis has already changed the way we operate, and some of those changes will be lasting. While we cannot eliminate one-on-one contact in human services, we are finding that there is a role for remote contact."

—Alan Mucatel, Chief Executive Officer, Rising Ground

Rising Ground provides essential services for families in the most need in the New York area. Not only did the organization experience significant cuts in funding, but it also saw rising costs as it provided even more essential goods to families, like diapers and food. The organization purchased cell phones and iPads to continue offering services to families remotely to reduce the risk of person-to-person transmission.

Even after much of the pandemic has decreased in risk, nonprofits will face a trend of continuing to safeguard interactions to prevent the spread of other diseases, colds, and viruses; ultimately, we may not be able to eliminate the COVID-19 virus entirely.

The global pandemic has challenged nonprofits like no other event in decades. At a time when beneficiaries need nonprofits the most, organizations are simultaneously challenged with private and government funding shortfalls and creating ways to protect staff, beneficiaries, and volunteers.

Staff

All employers have a duty to provide a safe and healthful workplace for employees under the Occupational Safety and Health Act (OSHA). In turn, OSHA relies on the Centers for Disease Control and Prevention (CDC), World Health Organization (WHO), National Institute of Occupational Health and Safety (NIOSH), and state and local public health authorities.

Employers are expected to develop an infectious disease outbreak response plan to protect staff and prevent an outbreak.[x] The plan includes:

- Conducting daily health checks.
- Doing a hazard assessment of the workplace.
- Encouraging employees to wear face coverings in the workplace.
- Implementing social distancing policies.
- Improving building ventilation systems.

The organization's plan must "cover all areas and job tasks with potential exposure to COVID-19 and control measures to eliminate or reduce such exposures."[xi]

Nonprofits have a duty to provide a safe working environment. OSHA requires an employer to provide a safe and healthful workplace for employees, and this likely extends to putting measures into place to protect workers from COVID-19.

Nonprofits need to be aware of their responsibility if a sick employee comes to work. There are strict rules regarding what employers can and cannot do concerning sick employees, and they should work with legal counsel to determine what controls should be in place for their particular situation. Generally, companies:

- May send employees home if they show COVID-19 symptoms.
- Should not require an employee to obtain medical care, even if they appear sick.
- Should provide reasonable accommodation in response to an employee inquiry related to COVID-19.
- May develop a respiratory protection program involving masks, as required by OSHA.
- May not place an employee on Family and Medical Leave Act if they are placed in an asymptomatic quarantine.

There are legal considerations with protecting your staff that every nonprofit should assess.

Employers should be prepared for long-term measures. We don't know when the pandemic will be generally considered as being finished. Still, experts believe COVID-19 may linger with the human population for some time to come, even popping up during the annual flu season as something we may need to continue contending with. If so, nonprofits should be prepared to have long-term measures in place to reduce the chance of spread.

Volunteers

Nonprofits should treat volunteers with the same care and process as they do employees to prevent the spread of viruses and disease. Putting these protocols in place will protect the health of staff, clients, and volunteers.

People want to help, and nonprofits shouldn't discourage volunteers. Instead, they can:

Communicate with volunteers. It's vital to communicate well with volunteers, especially in a time when volunteer opportunities are limited. Here are a few good tips for communicating with volunteers during a time when in-person volunteering is limited:

- Recognize and thank donors for their support.
- Set expectations with volunteers regarding the state of your programs and services, as well as your current needs.
- Be transparent with volunteers. They're committed to your beneficiaries and feel ownership in the organization.
- Let them know when you'll follow up with them.

You may find volunteers can help in other ways, such as donating, and will want to know what's going on with your organization. In fact, the 2020 Global Trends in Giving Survey found that 74% of volunteers donated to the organization they volunteer for.[xii]

Create guidelines for volunteering. It's crucial for you to create guidelines for your volunteers to know how your organization responds and what your expectations are for volunteers. Many of these guidelines will be similar to rules for staff. For example, if you offer in-person volunteer opportunities, you will include a policy that if a volunteer feels sick or has any symptoms, they should stay home. Guidelines will help volunteers understand the expectations for their involvement.

Create virtual volunteer opportunities. One way to reduce the risk of the spread of diseases is to create virtual volunteer opportunities. In a May 2020 survey of organizations regarding volunteerism, 45% reported creating new virtual volunteer opportunities.[xiii]

"During this time, we are finding new ways to connect with older New Yorkers so that their isolation does not spiral into loneliness and the physical and mental health declines that come along with it," said Kathryn Haslanger, CEO of JASA. "Loneliness was a growing public health crisis even before we were sheltering at home, and this pandemic has shed light on this critical need. In some ways, virtual activities can actually be more inclusive than in-person activities."

JASA has created new virtual groups and activities to include more seniors in their work. Developing virtual activities has increased the opportunity for people with walkers and wheelchairs.

If possible, nonprofits should explore ways for people to volunteer remotely.

Is virtual volunteering possible? Review your volunteer programs to see if a virtual experience is possible. For example, many literacy programs have created a virtual option to continue encouraging volunteers to connect with children. If it's not possible, move on to other ideas for how to involve volunteers.

Find skilled volunteers. With many volunteer programs shut down, it may be time to look for skilled volunteers to help, such as those with accounting or information technology experience. Many corporate giving programs have volunteer opportunities and are willing to allow staff to work remotely on projects. Contact the corporate social responsibility manager of a corporation you work with to see if there are opportunities.

Shortly after lockdowns happened, one local business offered up some of its staff to serve as volunteers for anything CRISTA needed, such as writing thank-you notes or stuffing envelopes. Businesses that support your organization may be encouraging volunteer time from staff.

Beneficiaries

Nonprofit beneficiaries encompass a wide range of people, services, and organizations, from individuals and families seeking basic needs to community youth centers to women seeking to start their own businesses. Maintaining meaningful interaction between nonprofits and those they serve is always essential, but it has become even more critical during the pandemic.

COVID has been an equal opportunity disruptor across the business spectrum, and nonprofits have felt the crunch. A survey from LaPiana Consulting found that by May 2020, 93% of nonprofit respondents had already been impacted in nearly every aspect. Organizations, both large and small, have made do with cut-backs in operational staff, reduced revenues, and more competition for corporate and individual donation dollars. But thanks to technology and a necessity-is-the-mother-of-invention willingness to adapt, nonprofits have been able to implement strategies to help safeguard their interactions with beneficiaries.

Ann Mond Johnson, CEO of the nonprofit American Telemedicine Association Health, notes that how before the pandemic the adoption rate of telehealth by consumers and healthcare professionals was low. But since the virus made social interaction a public health issue, telemedicine has become a fixture that will likely remain an integral part of interaction in the future.

"Physicians realize that in many instances, they could take care of the situation without actually laying hands on people. We have a bias of physicality in healthcare and what they found was that that was not necessary," Johnson says.

Sherry McAllister, President of the Foundation for Chiropractic Progress, says her nonprofit "developed and launched a campaign aimed at educating and supporting our members and the public on living their healthiest lives during these difficult times."

The lessons learned and systems implemented by these health and wellness organizations to maintain — and even improve — interacting with beneficiaries are applicable for nonprofits of all stripes.

Develop guidelines for how to interact with beneficiaries safely. Your organization must protect your beneficiaries from potential exposure to COVID-19 or any other potential health problem. The first step to help protect beneficiaries is to develop guidelines for how to interact with beneficiaries safely. The policies should address all details for how and when organizational staff will interact with beneficiaries.

Communicate with a purpose. The efforts to minimize the spread of COVID-19 have upended the usual ways of doing almost everything. Sheltering in place has meant a change in how services are provided. Making communication a priority will help keep beneficiaries informed, reduce the uncertainty that comes with change beyond our control, and assure people every effort is being made to meet their needs. But not all information is equal. It needs to be:

- Current with regular updates
- Relevant
- Clear and concise
- Available when the beneficiary needs it

Communicate across multiple platforms. Disseminating information on multiple platforms is the best way to reach as many beneficiaries as possible. Offer information in different formats — send out tip sheets via email, post a short e-book or brochure about new processes or procedures on a website, embed a video, or offer phone or video conferencing appointments for person-to-person contact, hosting a webinar — to increase engagement.

Establish education avenues to help beneficiaries adapt. While Zoom might be ubiquitous among white-collar employees who work from home, many casual Internet users are not necessarily familiar with how the app works. If you've had to move more aspects of your nonprofit online, establishing a phone helpline or online chat to answer questions in real-time will help beneficiaries stay engaged. Make sure to provide basic information, such as:

- Current days and hours of operation
- Services available
- Safety procedures, such as masks or limited capacity, implemented to ensure safety

- Contact information

Be proactive. The world is an incredibly fluid place right now and into the future, so not only have nonprofits' traditional ways of doing business changed, in many cases the beneficiaries' needs have as well. Nonprofits must have outreach initiatives to serve beneficiaries' concerns best and manage expectations if the nonprofit is shorthanded or unable to provide all services.

With feedback from beneficiaries, you gain an intimate understanding of their challenges and how your organization can better serve them. Further, this gives donors a more personal view into the lives they are impacting when giving to your cause.

An article in Stanford Social Innovation Review (SSIR) adds, "The importance of adaptability right now is apparent. Consider possible changes in client needs, behaviors, and the operating environment over the next six months and how your organization could respond. Bypassing the beneficiary as a source of information and experience [would] deprive ourselves of insights into how we might do better, insights that are uniquely grounded in the day-to-day experiences of the very people the programs are created for."

Interacting with beneficiaries has an added benefit for staff: when they can't be together in person, even virtual human interaction helps keep staff engaged.

Collaboration. The pandemic has created massive job loss. School closures have forced many parents — often women — to quit their jobs to stay home and care for and tutor their children. Many nonprofits in the social sector, such as those that provide food or clothing, have been inundated with people in need. To maintain their ability to interact with beneficiaries, many nonprofits with complementary services teamed up. By sharing resources, the organizations can reach and interact with more people and take on larger projects they wouldn't be able to independently.

In any time of crisis — economic downturns, wars, natural disasters, pandemics — the organizations that prove the most resilient, maintain strong interactions with their beneficiaries, and provide a safe workplace for staff all have strong leadership. Emphasizing frequent and transparent communications alongside best practices creates a productive, sustainable culture that will safeguard interactions and relationships with the beneficiaries and stakeholders they serve.

Nimble Program Delivery

"Our principle is to build the plane as you fly because this is the time of crisis," said Muhammed Musa, Executive Director of BRAC International.

Before the crisis, BRAC partnered with the LEGO Foundation to create play-based learning labs to address children's emotional, social, and psychological needs in learning. Once the pandemic hit, the in-person learning model was shut down, and the organization quickly pivoted to digital learning labs delivered via mobile devices provided by the organization to children and families.

BRAC discovered the need to pivot programs to a different delivery model to continue helping people during a pandemic. Some of the ideas the organization is exploring won't be successful, but through consistent testing and revisions, the successes will result in new ways for students to learn.

Lesson: The flexible nonprofit survives. The pandemic demonstrated to many nonprofit organizations the need for more nimble programs.

In 2017, the Wallace Foundation studied 45 nonprofit social programs to determine the strategic decisions that led to successful program scaling. Through a combination of reviewing program documentation, interviews, and in-depth studies of four programs, Wallace determined that organizations need to answer three key areas: how to scale ("pathways"), whom to involve ("partnerships"), and retention of program quality ("fidelity").[xiv]

These three core areas for program scaling are relevant to today's nonprofits challenged with nimble program delivery. When an organization designs, or even reinvents, a program to scale up or down, it provides the necessary flexibility to deal with unpredictable funding.

The pandemic has demonstrated the need for flexibility in how nonprofits deliver services. With a forced economic shutdown, many programs and services had to be closed quickly. The shutdown was global, so the need to pivot was felt and understood by stakeholders in the process. But what if the program shutdown, or even service expansion, was localized to one area or a single nonprofit? How quickly can the nonprofit organization make the change? How does the organization communicate the change to stakeholders?

How to Scale

Scaling nonprofit programs isn't a simple process. Scaling up programs requires efficiencies to ensure the program outcome benefits outweigh the implementation costs. For example, programs often need a certain number of people to start with staffing efficiencies as the program expands. If the organization doesn't receive efficiencies at scale, it may not be feasible to grow a program beyond a certain level.

The post-pandemic nonprofit also needs to design programs that can be scaled down, or contracted, during lean times. Contracting programs presents a new level of challenges, as your organization likely has a fixed cost to consider when implementing programs.

As you consider how to scale programs, up or down, you'll likely ask yourself these questions:

- How will we adapt our programs to increase flexibility?
- Who can lead these efforts?
- How do we fund nimble programs?
- Who will execute the programs?

Agile Program Leadership

If your organization wants to create nimble programs, you need deft leadership. The leader's agility level in the face of changing conditions is one of the primary factors in determining the successful scaling or contracting of a program.

Agile leaders must know when to start and stop specific programs. The post-pandemic nonprofit needs program leadership that can adapt and change to market conditions. Leadership should design programs that can be activated and deactivated on command and hibernate for periods of time if required. Hibernating a program may not even be pandemic-related. There may be funding problems, staff issues, or political concerns, for just a few examples, that require work to be stopped or started at will.

Many grants can take months to get started, and during a renewal period, it may be necessary to pause an active program while the funding for the grant is in process. During this time, a skeleton staff (or perhaps no staff at all) is required, but the program itself cannot be shut down entirely. It must be placed into hibernation to be reactivated once funding has come through. Agile program leaders design services or programs that can be activated and deactivated.

Funding Scalable Programs

A challenge for many nonprofits is the perception that an organization is measured based only on the dollars invested into specific programs with little reporting of long-term impact. The immediate challenge for the organization's fundraisers is to raise money for the programs the organization is currently implementing, with little ability to raise funds for prospective programs. Large funding organizations such as foundations or government grant-makers want to know precisely what the money will be used for and the anticipated results — often without paying any overhead costs. Private donors want a thank-you note within two days and a story of impact a couple weeks after the donation. This leaves little ability to fund creative ideas that could help scale programs.

This is why many nonprofits are turning to new sources for funding such as crowdfunding, membership dues, and corporate sponsorships to maintain their mission sustainably.

- Crowdfunding via specialized websites allows donors to give small increments over time with little risk involved; it also builds community buy-in.
- Recurring donors regularly give to support nonprofit programs – a popular option for nonprofits to activate their most loyal donors.
- Membership dues are a sustainable revenue source for organizations because people commit to paying monthly or annually and don't usually cancel their membership.
- Corporate sponsorships can be in the form of donations, sponsorship advertising on nonprofit branding materials (such as websites or newsletters), and product placement at events that align with corporate values.

Beyond new income sources, nonprofits should also approach large funders about providing additional funding for new initiatives. During the pandemic, many funders offered to change restricted funding to unrestricted to help provide the most flexibility for grant recipients. With the right business case, some funders may be willing to provide grants for your organization to create nimble programs.

How Do We Drive Outcomes?

Our organization desires a positive outcome for beneficiaries. Whether it's a hungry person getting something to eat, a child receiving an education, the enjoyment of a patron experiencing an opera, or an animal cared for, we desire that our programs result in something positive. In the post-pandemic world, we need to be prepared to scale our programs up or down but still achieve positive outcomes for our beneficiaries.

How do we continue to drive positive outcomes?

Nonprofit leaders will be challenged to decide how programs will be implemented and who will implement them. Studies have found that the decision about who implements a program dramatically determines whether or not an organization will successfully scale a program.

There are three types of program implementors: self, affiliates, and third-party networks.

Self-implementation. At Food for the Hungry, many programs are implemented by the organization's capacity. For example, FH started using savings groups in communities decades ago. As the organization refined the savings group model, it implemented the methodology in other countries until every country it worked in had some form of community savings groups. When an organization designs the program, distributes, and implements it, it is using branching pathways.

This is a straightforward process for scaling programs and gives an organization the most flexibility. As the program developer and implementer, your organization will directly control a program's growth or contraction using the methods you design. This is especially important for complex programs where you have tight controls to ensure program quality.

Affiliates. In the corporate sector, businesses have long used franchising as a method of duplicating systems, processes, and distribution. In the nonprofit sector, the closest model to franchising is affiliates. Affiliates are field organizations that license the rights to programs from a lead organization. An example of an affiliate organization is Make-a-Wish. The lead organization manages the brand and program development while the local affiliates are responsible for fundraising and implementation for their region. Often, there is a legal contract regarding branding, program quality, and funding that the affiliate organization must adhere to. Compared to the self-implementation model, having affiliates reduces financial risk for the lead organization as it puts both funding and staffing responsibility on the affiliate partner. The lead organization can quickly scale a program up or down since the affiliate is responsible for implementation.

The lead organization loses some control over program implementation and quality. The affiliate may not execute precisely the desired way, and it's difficult for the lead partner to monitor and enforce outcomes.

Third-party networks. A third-party network is an existing nonprofit organization with its own infrastructure to implement programs. For example, your organization might develop a program implemented through an organization such as the YMCA or Boys & Girls Clubs of America. The lead organization designs and supports the program while the third-party network distributes and implements it to beneficiaries.

Often, the lead organization modifies the program to fit the distribution partner's local agencies best. Sometimes feedback from the local agency is incorporated into the design iteration process of the program. In this model, the lead organization has the least control over how the program is implemented and the specific outcomes but often has a significant reach that would otherwise be unavailable. The lead organization might reach more people than they could on their own.

Selecting a path. However your organization currently operates — self-implementation, affiliates, or third-party networks — the pandemic provides an opportunity to evaluate if your operating model is the best for moving forward as a nimble nonprofit. As your organization considers your current model and other potential models, it's helpful to ask these questions:

1. Do we currently have the flexibility to scale or contract our programs?
2. How does our current operating model affect the success of scaling our programs?
3. Can we positively impact beneficiary outcomes by adopting or adding a different program implementation model?

Maintaining Program Quality

When a nonprofit organization is forced to scale a program up or down, a primary concern is its quality. When you scale a program too far down, program implementers are concerned with having sufficient resources to achieve their goals. When you scale a program up, implementers are worried about maintaining quality and effectiveness for program outcomes. A goal when scaling programs to be a nimble nonprofit is consistent program delivery.

According to the Wallace Foundation research, there are two primary methods for scaling a program: reinvention and adaptation. An organization may choose to reinvent programs to increase chances for scaling. Second, implementors working with beneficiaries may adapt programs. The nonprofit organization has less control over what implementors do, potentially impacting program quality. One or both of these methods may be involved with scaling a program.

Reinvention

Brigadoon Village, Canada's largest pediatric illness camp, canceled camp activities during the pandemic. Unfortunately, 800 children missed out on camp activities. The organization created a "Virtual Village" to deliver programs online to give the kids a sense of community.

Likewise, CRISTA Camps had to cancel the 2020 camping season, impacting hundreds of campers. The organization began offering virtual camp experiences and started the Miracle Horse Club, an innovative monthly donor program to fund the care of the camp's horses during the pandemic.

An organization may choose to reinvent programs to scale more efficiently. Reinvention occurs at the lead organization and could include feedback from implementers working directly with beneficiaries. Though an organization could opt to forgo input from implementers, including such information could provide valuable insight about how a program operates.

For example, World Vision successfully feeds millions of children every year through a combination of cash, vouchers, and food boxes. The organization found that many children only received a full meal at school and would use up vouchers quickly each month. The organization changed the program to provide two food vouchers per child at school each day and found better outcomes.

The food voucher program is an excellent example of successful reinvention because it increased effectiveness by fulfilling identified needs, which helped children eat healthier meals every day. Nonprofits need to remain flexible so they can continue meeting goals or address specific needs as they arise.

Organizations reinvent programs to increase the likelihood of successful implementation.

Create an innovation strategy. Consider how the current program operates to develop a plan for improvements. Also, consider whether there are any partnerships through which creativity may flow more freely by collaborating with another group outside the organization.

Set goals. What are the objectives of this program? Clearly define your goal or mission to determine how you can continue achieving it while being flexible enough that new ideas for change will come up as they're needed and not be forced into a corner with no options left.

Identify your program's strengths. Build on existing strengths to find opportunities for improvement. Consider whether an innovative solution is already working somewhere within your organization but needs some tweaking before it can be scaled across the board — this could be managerial approach, programming content, or delivery system, as well as things you may not have considered at all.

Identify an internal champion. Find an internal champion of innovation who can help other people in the organization understand that reinventing programs is about fixing what's broken and identifying new opportunities such as expanding their program into another geographic area or country. The more people inside the organization who favor strategic improvements, the easier it will be to promote change initiatives.

Be flexible. Be flexible in your approach when it comes to doing things differently or developing new ideas for helping more donors and beneficiaries: "One good idea does not an organization make, but one bad idea wastes resources on ineffective approaches forevermore," cautions Dr. John Foushi from Johns Hopkins Bloomberg School of Public Health's Department of Population Sciences.

Innovation can happen at any point in time, but it's not a light switch that one person flips on then waits for others in the organization to catch up. It's a messy and often uncomfortable process that requires patience from all stakeholders. Nonprofits should take a leap; they need their own permission slip before embarking on this journey so that they have enough space, flexibility, and latitude as they innovate their programs while taking care along the way not to hurt themselves or those who work alongside them. Nonprofit leaders must show a willingness to innovate and be open-minded about looking for new ways to help more donors or beneficiaries.

Adaptation

In contrast to reinvention, adaptation occurs closest to the beneficiary. The program implementor adapts a program to be more effective with a client. Though these adaptations may be seemingly small changes, with enough small changes the impact on program design can be considerable.

Develop a needs assessment. The first thing to do is conduct a needs assessment and talk with the people you serve about what they need.

A needs assessment is the process of evaluating a program or service to determine whether it meets the identified need effectively.

An example of this might be conducting a survey, focus group, interview study, or using other tools like cognitive interviews that identify strengths and weaknesses within existing programs, services, and policies. The results are used to inform decision-making about what change efforts should be made for the future. Nonprofit organizations can use these findings to improve their programming strategies to better address beneficiaries' needs while also achieving organizational goals. One organization found out from its beneficiary feedback that they were not addressing specific topics enough during one-on-ones with clients because they didn't know which ones would be most useful; after incorporating those topics in their programs, they saw a spike in the number of clients who sought out one-on-ones.

Not every program is scalable the way it was designed. An essential part of this process is understanding that not all communities are identical; some will need adaptations relative to others.

One nonprofit found that its program was not well suited for those it was designed to serve; after finding this out from beneficiary feedback, they decided to stop the project instead of trying another approach. This allowed them more time and money, which could be used elsewhere or donated back into the community so that other organizations could continue serving people with similar needs.

Another organization adapted its program based on what beneficiaries said about where and when they wanted programming delivered — people told them they were interested in receiving services at work, so programs pivoted to be offered during lunch hours or before/after shifts. This has allowed the clientele to be reachable with these new offerings as opposed to just pursuing individual clients who show up outside business hours. Adapting can be critical for nonprofits when a program isn't initially achieving goals.

Many nonprofits do not operate from one playbook when it comes to providing services but instead rely heavily on adapting what they're doing to work better for beneficiaries. In the post-pandemic world, nonprofits need scalable programs to have the flexibility to achieve their goals.

Nonprofit organizations must have the ability to adapt and thrive in a changing environment. With supporters and beneficiaries expecting more from their nonprofits, nonprofit leaders must develop organizational agility.

Logistics & Travel Constraints

When tropical storm Harold struck the island nation of Vanuatu in April 2020, World Hope International typically would have sent a team of volunteers to provide drinking water to tens of thousands of people. But this time, travel restrictions prevented the organization from responding.

Charities Aid Foundation of America found in its survey, *The Voices of Charities Facing COVID-19 Worldwide*, that 70.5% of charities reported travel restrictions disrupted their contact with donors and beneficiaries.[xv]

After the pandemic started, most countries implemented controls on the free movement of people and goods across borders. These restrictions negatively impacted nonprofits that enjoyed such movement of staff and goods. Unfortunately, we are unlikely to return to the pre-pandemic state of free movement in the next several years.

Country Border Restrictions

As the world slowly emerges from the COVID-19 pandemic, people are faced with a new reality that many things will not return to normal anytime soon, one of which is travel. The pre-COVID world was one of travel waivers, affordable and relatively quick international flights, and the easy flow of people, money, and goods across borders. Before the pandemic, the ease of travel was helpful for various nonprofit and non-governmental organizations. Now, these organizations are forced to reevaluate their cross-border strategies.

Many countries have limitations on international travel and, at the very least, require those entering their countries to be tested for COVID-19. The United States, certain European Union countries, and the United Kingdom and Ireland all have similar travel restrictions, limiting entrance from certain countries and requiring COVID-19 testing and possible quarantine. The UK requires its citizens to be tested when reentering the country.

The reality of renewed travel restrictions looks like a real possibility, but how will nonprofit organizations survive under these conditions? Nonprofits with an international reach have to reassess staffing and shipping goods across borders. Localization may be in the best interest of all nonprofits, as it could help them thrive while dealing with new laws.

Expats may have a more difficult time getting work permits. Nearly every nation-state in the world has reacted to the COVID-19 by limiting the number of visas given to those entering.

Compounding the work visa limitation problem is the fact that many consulates and visa application centers have been closed. An international relief organization recently shared the story of a staff member in Ecuador and the struggle acquiring a work visa. The embassy's website states a 999-day delay, though it may be much longer — the office has been closed since March 2020. The backlog of applications in 2020 will certainly cause significant delays.

In some countries, elected officials and government agencies have helped acquire work visas on an emergency basis. Consult with your local representatives to determine if your nonprofit can obtain a work visa through alternative channels.

Nonprofits will need to hire more local staff. The international travel limitations caused by the COVID-19 pandemic will continue to cause staffing problems for many organizations. Work visa restrictions limit the pool of potential staff to local people. Internationally focused nonprofits will find more difficulties attracting experienced staff with international backgrounds for leadership roles.

In the next several years, international nonprofit organizations will have to adapt and learn how to better utilize local, regional, and national talent pools for all employment levels.

Free movement of people during disasters will be limited. Those in nonprofit management, especially nonprofits that function internationally, will have to adjust to the new reality that the free movement of people during disasters will be significantly curtailed. This trend started before COVID-19, with countries like Indonesia limiting foreign citizens from entering regions after a natural disaster. When you combine these policies with the limitations put in place within the pandemic, we should see an increase in restrictions during a disaster. These restrictions could negatively impact relief efforts during the next earthquake or hurricane.

Locally registered organizations have more success moving people during disasters. If registering your nonprofit locally is not an option, your organization should look for a local partner to assist during a natural disaster.

Shipping goods will face delays. The United Nations Conference on Trade and Development estimates that cross-border investments will be reduced by up to 40% in 2021,[xvi] which means the flow of goods will be severely restricted. The primary reason for this is the COVID-19 pandemic, but the situation has been exasperated by populist-inspired trade policies in many countries that promote tariffs, customs controls, and protectionism in general.

The trend of increased local, regional, and national production of goods shows no signs of slowing. Nonprofits that have traditionally packed goods in shipping containers in the U.S. to other countries may find local acquisition is quicker and cheaper than waiting for customs clearance.

Regional Goods Production

In Sri Lanka, the Red Cross created a research and development team to design and produce personal protection equipment (PPE) for frontline workers using locally sourced raw materials. By manufacturing PPE locally, the Red Cross drove costs from $20 to only $3.

As border restrictions were put in place in 2020, the free movement of goods between countries slowed down — even stopped — and it became difficult to get specific types of goods. Some countries banned the export of critical medical supplies, drugs, or vaccines until their own country had enough. The result was more regionalized production to provide for local demand and allow countries to be less dependent on open global trade.

Many countries have become more protectionist, adding in tariffs and restrictions to slow down trade. This has forced more regional production to fulfill market demand. This won't slow down in the post-pandemic world; in fact, it may increase.

How does this impact the post-pandemic nonprofit?

Shipping certain types of gifts-in-kind will become more challenging. Acquiring certain types of medical supplies and drugs during the pandemic became more difficult. In the future, countries may slow down or prevent these goods from shipping, and some countries may seize these goods upon entry to be used as the government sees fit. It may be more reliable for these organizations to acquire goods locally or build local distribution centers for easier product movement between countries in different regions.

Regional production will benefit some countries. A benefit for regionalized production is the potential for new jobs to come to areas that have long suffered from a lack of employment. As tariffs and trade restrictions are put in place, it will force production to become more regional and create new employment opportunities in those areas. With more employment will come increased economic activity and (hopefully) lift people out of poverty. Organizations may find their work shifting in these areas.

Faster Move to Localization

Localization, a buzzword in international NGOs over the past several years, is set to become a much larger force internationally and domestically in the years to come. Localization refers to the preference of funders to invest in local nonprofit organizations in the belief that people closer to the community will have better insight into the programs and services necessary to accomplish a goal. The effort has a noble purpose: get the money closest to the people who need it most.

Some would argue that local NGOs don't have the scale or experience that larger organizations do. There is greater risk in funding local NGOs, as record-keeping, metrics, and program effectiveness are difficult for smaller nonprofits to manage.

Countries are also seeing value in having local nonprofit organizations invest in local communities. Country leadership believes a local NGO will hire local staff and inject more money into the communities where they work.

This challenge is even coming to domestic organizations in the United States as more grants are being made available to local organizations serving in communities around the country instead of larger block grants made to country-wide organizations.

Benefits to localization. As much as the COVID-19 pandemic has brought numerous difficulties to nonprofits concerning international staffing and the logistics of long-distance supply chains, there is room for organizations to take advantage of the situation. Although born out of necessity, the move toward localization may have numerous benefits for nonprofit organizations, especially when listening to and executing local needs. The transition to localization also means that organizations will have to reach out to local experts and better utilize resources and institutions in the local community.

Therefore, the transition to localization may strengthen local relationships, which will enhance communities. After all, the primary goal of every nonprofit is to help others and build better communities.

It should be pointed out that the trend toward localization isn't necessarily something new, with many nonprofit organizations having been moving in this direction for several years. A key benefit to localization is increased community involvement in working toward positive outcomes. What works in Rwanda may not work in Haiti. This is why it is imperative to listen and work more closely with locals.

Nonprofits and NGOs may have access to more resources and better technology that may help fulfill a mission, but the locals those resources are intended to help know the customs, culture, and people of their countries better, so local workers' perspectives will be crucial to the success of any endeavor.[xvii]

Another notable benefit of localization for organizations to consider is in the area of funding. Studies show that localization in funding is more flexible, resulting in long-term commitments that are more conducive to organizational success. Localization in funding has also proven to be more efficient, with at least 25% of all funding directly reaching the people who need it.[xviii]

The last point brings attention to a dilemma that many organizations, for-profit and nonprofits alike, face in their day-to-day operations: red tape. No matter the country, red tape is always the same: the proverbial layer upon layer of bureaucratic rules, regulations, and workers whose duty is to enforce those rules and regulations. Although localization cannot eliminate red tape, it can mitigate the problems associated with it by giving local workers, who know local officials and laws, more responsibilities in organizations.

Create a locally registered organization. With all these restrictions on travel, visas, and even the movement of goods across borders, nonprofits will have to think locally if they want to keep a footprint in multiple countries. Nonprofits may have to register locally in countries where they intend to successfully deliver services to beneficiaries in order to navigate this new reality. When a nonprofit decides to establish a branch or chapter of its organization in another country, it will essentially function as a separate organization with a unique government registration and locals on the board of directors. When nonprofits establish semi-autonomous branches of their organizations in other countries, there are some notable benefits.

The primary benefit of this arrangement is that local employees of nonprofits will be better able to communicate with local officials, who usually favor locally registered organizations. A local footprint will also allow nonprofits to acquire grants, loans, and other funding that are only available to in-country registered organizations. Finally, local branches of nonprofits can help carry out organizations' mission statements by working directly with locals who need the aid.

Despite numerous positives that come with nonprofit organizations registering locally in other countries, some drawbacks must be considered.

With the autonomy that this type of set-up brings to the locally established branches of the nonprofit, the issue of control, or lack thereof, should be considered. The local board of directors in the locally established branches have a great deal of power and can essentially do as they want. If this becomes a problem, the directors of the primary organization can cut funding to a branch, but this, or even the threat of reduced funding, should only be a last resort.

The key to avoiding problems with locally registered branches of nonprofits is to keep clear and open lines of communication. The mission statement of the lead organization should be known and repeated by all workers, no matter the country they are in. In addition, the idea that everyone is part of a larger team should be emphasized.

Work with partners. Many nonprofits don't have the resources or time to establish a locally registered branch of their organization in another country. It takes a lot of time and money to carry out such an endeavor, and if this wasn't done before the COVID-19 pandemic it would undoubtedly be complicated to do so today.

Nonprofit organizations could also establish partnerships with existing nonprofits in the localities in which they want to serve.

One benefit to establishing a partnership with a separate nonprofit in another country is logistical. Your organization will not have to worry about obtaining work visas for workers and won't have to register with local authorities to establish a new branch of your organization. This scenario also results in little to no expenses for staff and overhead.

Since the organization your nonprofit will be working with is an independent entity and not a subsidiary, your local control over the mission is very limited. As much as controlling the local board of directors may be difficult in the first scenario, it is always a possibility as long as you still control the "purse strings." When you are working with a partner, your organization doesn't have authority over the independent nonprofit organization. Your organization may find it challenging to get up-to-date videos, photos, and stories.

There are steps you can take to mitigate such problems.

The key to maintaining a good relationship between organizations is open communication. Despite potentially being separated by thousands of miles, you're still able to communicate instantly via phones, Skype, or other messaging services. Email updates can also keep partners informed on what is happening.

Nonprofit organizations should vet any local partners they choose to work with. An excellent local partner should share the same mission as your organization and come with an excellent reputation. You can find this information through interagency working groups, charity rating services, and local officials.

Building solid relationships with local nonprofits can help your organization maximize resources, get more work accomplished, and expand your reach.

The travel restrictions associated with the COVID-19 pandemic will eventually pass, but future global pandemics or disasters may create a replay of what we have already experienced. Nonprofits that have developed localized networks in the countries they serve will be better equipped to handle future restrictions.

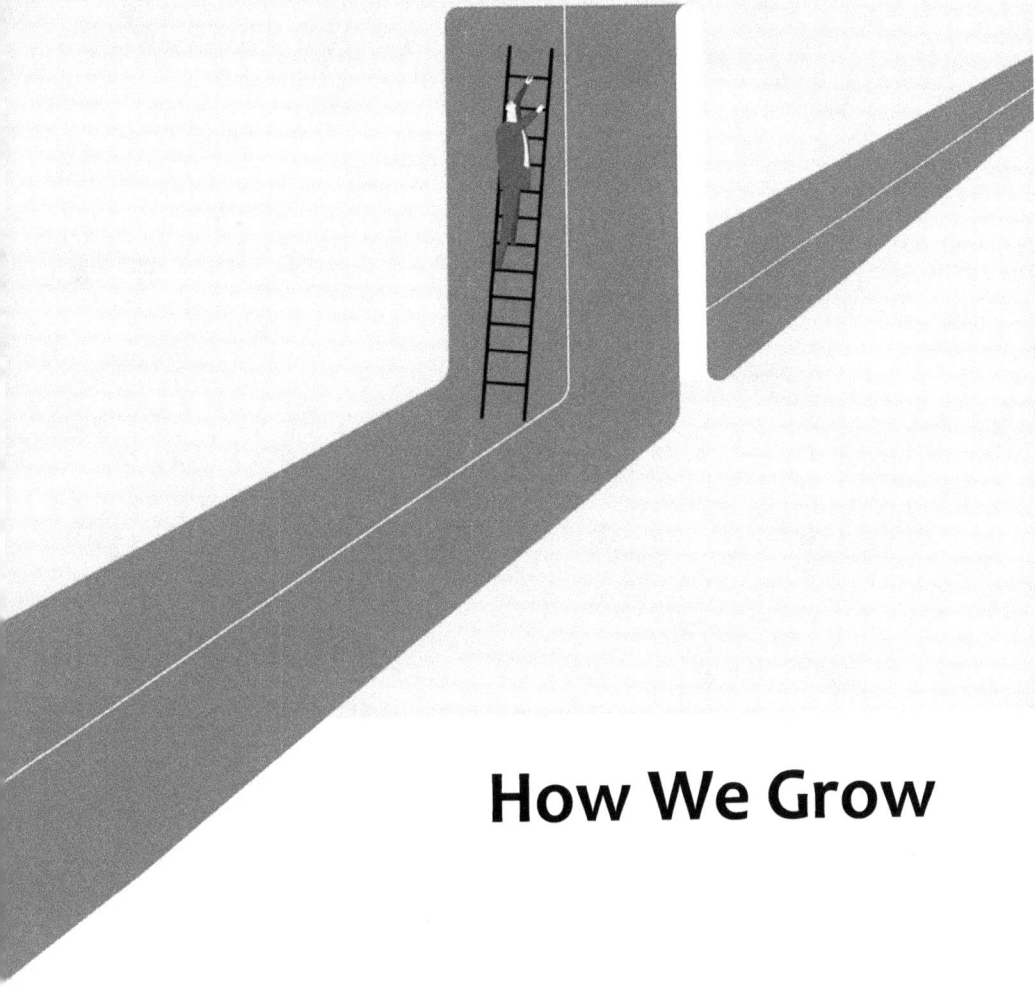

How We Grow

How Will Giving Change?

"The pandemic has forced many nonprofit organizations to overhaul fundraising plans and seek new funding sources as they face potential city and state budget cuts and the loss of other previously reliable funding streams," remarked Lisa David of Public Health Solutions, when discussing how the pandemic is impacting her organization. "Now more than ever, individual and corporate donor support is essential."

For many nonprofits, 2020 was an exceptional year in fundraising. However, the pandemic still represents an existential threat for nonprofit organizations.

That's not hyperbole. There are no guarantees in what the short-term future looks like. If a global economic slowdown begins for several years, nonprofit organizations will face funding challenges like never before. Short-term governmental economic interventions will end, and economies will contract. Unfortunately, this will lead to many organizations closing their doors.

During this time, giving will change. Let's discuss a few of those changes and how they will impact your organization.

Rejuvenation of Direct Mail

Not only is direct mail giving stable, but it also increased in 2020. Direct mail donations have increased 4.9% year over year, with average gifts increasing 23.5%.[xix] People are home during the pandemic and reading the mail nonprofit organizations (and, increasingly, for-profit corporations) are sending. Many are responding. There is circumstantial evidence that direct mail is driving more people to give digitally. If a donor runs out of stamps, what will motivate her to stand in line at the post office when she can simply give online?

Each year in the nonprofit industry, some pundits want to declare that direct mail is dead. Yet the numbers don't tell that story. Organizations that embrace a vibrant direct mail program find it can be one of the channels you use for a successful mix of fundraising.

Where is direct mail going? The price for personalizing mail continues to drop as donors prefer a more one-to-one relationship with a nonprofit. Sixty percent of donors value a personalized experience with their nonprofit, while only 41% feel like they're receiving that experience. For example, adding a name to a direct mail letter can increase response by 135%.[xx] Nonprofits will develop programs and acquire tools to create a more personalized experience for donors, including direct mail.

What about donor acquisition through direct mail? Donor acquisition works in direct mail. World Concern launched a direct mail donor acquisition campaign in July 2020 — in the middle of the pandemic — and saw tremendous success in both the percentage that converted and the average gift amount. In fact, 14% of the donors acquired in July had given a second gift by October 2020, just three months after their first gift. Most nonprofits are excited for a 25% second-year renewal rate during the first year a donor is on file.

Direct mail acquisition can be an expensive channel if you only measure the initial return on investment. However, if you properly cultivate these donors, they can become some of your most loyal givers and provide a foundation of income for the organization. A key we've found to increasing donor loyalty is to provide opportunities for them to give in multiple channels.

Vibrant Digital Giving

The biggest benefactor this year for giving may be digital channels. The 2020 Global Trends in Giving Survey captured this trend among COVID-19 donors and found that 80.5% of those surveyed preferred to give online.[xxi]

Donors expect a smooth user experience. Your donors use major Internet retailers and experience a fast and easy-to-use checkout system. They get products in a few hours delivered to their doorstep. They have user-friendly mobile apps. Donors now expect your website to offer information about how their donation will be used to make an impact and change someone's life — *and* an easy way to donate. As donors rely on more digital experiences for every aspect of their lives, from shopping to exercise to entertainment, the antiquated giving experience from their favorite nonprofit will no longer be acceptable. But your donor won't complain to you about it. She will simply leave and find another organization to support. This organization tells compelling stories and provides a simple way to give from any device. This organization reports back to the donor and demonstrates how her gift was used effectively and produced excellent results.

If your digital presence is stuck in the past, you must update it and provide a meaningful and smooth user experience.

Video is a vital part of your marketing mix. Over the past few years, video has been an essential tool in the nonprofit marketer's toolkit. In the near future, nonprofits will be expected to offer videos that demonstrate the good work donors are giving toward. It will be a vital part of your marketing mix — without it, your organization will have a difficult time connecting with donors in a meaningful way.

Why?

Consumers expect video from brands since the medium tells a story with more clarity than written word. As consumers increasingly expect nonprofits to tell them what was accomplished with their donations, video will be the standard for high-impact storytelling.

Personalized videos will be commonplace. A few years ago, I signed up for an email marketing service, and a couple of days after signing up, I received a personal video message from the company's president. He started out calling me by name and welcoming me as a new customer. He talked a bit about why they do what they do and offered to help me if I had any problems. The experience was so compelling and memorable that I shared it with my dinner guests that evening.

Personalized video services have been used in corporations for some time but have been slower to be adopted by nonprofits. However, personalized videos welcoming new donors and used as a channel for major donor communications will grow in the post-pandemic world.

These services allow representatives from your organization to create a custom-made video using their phone, tablet, or laptop and automatically send it to a donor, supporter, or volunteer. These services help endear a supporter to the organization. *Someone from this organization took the time to send me a video personally?*

Organizations that integrate these videos into their welcome process and major giving areas will see donors who engage with the organization at higher rates and stay longer.

Increased Multi-Channel Giving

According to the *State of Multi-Channel Donor Communications* report from NextAfter and Virtuous, the average revenue from multi-channel donors was $494 per year compared to $159, $301, and $148 for offline-only, offline with a valid email address on file, and online-only donors respectively.[xxii] The report also shows that multi-channel donors are loyal donors. Donor renewal jumps from 43% for offline donors and 36% for online donors to 67% for multi-channel donors. The Blackbaud Institute found that donor retention for multi-channel donors is double that of single-channel donors. When you have donors giving in more than one channel, you create more loyal donors who give more over time.

To increase this all-important multi-channel giving, nonprofit organizations can adopt several simple strategies.

Call donors to welcome them. It's vital for any nonprofit to develop effective, long-lasting relationships with donors. A welcome call is an effective way to demonstrate gratitude to a new donor and start building a relationship. It helps with donor retention and reduces donor remorse.

If your nonprofit organization doesn't have a dedicated donor care team, you can perform welcome calls using team members across departments, volunteers, or the board of directors.

Send a welcome series. After your organization gains a new donor, it's vital to welcome the donor well. Sending an email welcome series to a new donor will increase the likelihood she will give again. It can also encourage donors in mail or radio to give digitally. The typical new donor welcome series is three to four emails in length with a week between each:

1. A gratitude email demonstrating how much you appreciate the donation.

2. Trust-building email with an impact story.
3. Video or engagement email.
4. Second appeal for an additional gift.

The welcome series should be personalized to the acquisition channel or type of donation. Develop a welcome series for single gift donors and recurring donors. Build a different email welcome series for a donor giving to clean water than one giving to education. Personalizing your welcome series demonstrates to donors that you value their gifts.

Be sure to send the first email within 48 hours of receiving a donation. Most nonprofits that implement welcome series use a marketing tool to send the series after a first-time donation automatically.

Follow up with a "thank you" card. After my first donation to Medical Teams International, a volunteer sent me a handwritten thank-you card. Unfortunately, few organizations follow the model of Medical Teams International and send these cards.

A thank-you card will deepen the relationship with a donor and increase the likelihood of receiving a second gift. When you create a timely thank-you that explains the impact the donor made and makes the donor feel genuinely appreciated, you've created something relevant and meaningful to the donor. The heartfelt thank-you should be custom and specific to the donation, not a boilerplate message.

If you're thanking the donor for money, mention how it will be put to good use. If they donated their time, explain precisely what kind of help they gave and what that meant to your organization. If you can, include something personal about yourself and your connection to the organization. Consider adding an open-ended question or something about your nonprofit that allows them to share more information with you. This will create a connection and opportunity for conversation when they receive the card!

Demonstrate impact to the donor. It's easy to use industry jargon in our communications or generalize how the donor is helping. It doesn't contribute to the donor relationship to tell the donor the gift provided "hope." It would be best if you were more specific. Explaining the impact in the thank-you communication helps build trust with the donor that your organization will do good work with the gifts she makes.

What do I mean when I say to "explain the impact"?

First, let's look at an example of a poorly worded thank-you I received.

"Your $35 donation for Emergency Response has been received. Your donation to Nonprofit Org, a 501c(3) tax-deductible organization, is tax-deductible as provided by law. Your donation is appreciated."

Tell a beneficiary story or provide a specific example of how the donor's gift will be used. For example, "Thank you for your $35 donation to our emergency response fund. Right now, we're rushing aid to refugees in the Middle East, and your gift will help provide emergency supplies, food, and shelter for one family." You may not be able to tell the donor where her donation will be used explicitly, but you can give a general idea of the impact she made.

Use text messaging to engage a donor. While the average email open rate is 33%, SMS messaging has an open rate of 99%, with 97% of messages opened within the first 15 minutes. Email click-thru rates average 6%, while 36% of people click-thru on an SMS message. Text messaging is an excellent channel to engage existing donors and re-engage lapsed donors.

How are nonprofits using text messaging? To:

1. Keep the supporter informed of upcoming events and campaigns.
2. Increase digital giving with targeted giving opportunities.
3. Keep volunteers engaged in between volunteer opportunities.
4. Show gratitude after a donation or volunteering time.

Cause-Oriented Giving Reduces Donor Loyalty

One challenging generational-driven change is donors are increasingly becoming less loyal to organizations and more interested in causes. The silent generation and baby boomers have loyalty to specific organizations, while millennials and generation Z are more cause-oriented. For example, a younger donor may care about clean water and care less about a particular organization, giving to multiple clean water organizations throughout the year.

Reinforce trust with the donor. One way to combat the loss of donor loyalty is to establish your organization as trustworthy. Your nonprofit gains the confidence of a supporter by demonstrating that the organization accomplishes what it says it will.

Lifewater International, a 40-year-old clean water-focused nonprofit, lets donors choose precisely where they want to donate and then reports back on the progress of that clean water project. For example, I can donate today to Nalongo, Uganda, where 56 families, or 210 people, are waiting for clean water.

On each project page, Lifewater provides more information to help show you the organization is trustworthy. One section shares the latest project news, while another shows milestones of the progress made. You can explore the community through an interactive map. The fundraiser includes a goal and shows you the donors who recently gave to the project.

All these points of information help encourage donors to see the organization as trustworthy. Develop clear messages about what your organization does, who you work with, how you work, and the impact donors make on the cause.

Tell stories of impact. When a donor gives a gift to your organization, a story loop is opened. The story begins with your donor being a hero to a beneficiary, and then explaining what the gift is used for closes the loop with that donor. If you don't close this loop, she will wonder what her contribution was used for. If you don't share this information, your donor may create assumptions to fill in the gaps you're not filling.

Children International, an international development nonprofit focused on children, shares hundreds of impact stories on its blog at https://www.children.org/stories. These stories often include powerful videos that explain a story in a much more effective way than simply using text.

Create "wow" moments with donors. "Wow" moments help a donor feel connected to your organization. Surprising donors with demonstrations of gratitude and showing how much they're appreciated helps them build a relationship with your organization.

After I'd made a donation to a college student support ministry, I received a phone call from the Executive Director thanking me for the gift and asking if there was anything he could do for me. One of the students in the ministry sent me a handwritten thank-you card. These two "wow" moments turned me into a lifelong donor.

In donor psychology, there is a concept called "reciprocity." When you do something for a donor, she feels like she needs to reciprocate and perform an action for you.

Even small tokens of appreciation can bring goodwill from donors, increasing trust and retention.

Supporters want to know, like, and trust an organization before they commit. With public trust in nonprofit organizations waning, building an organization that is trustworthy will increase connectedness between an organization and its donors, staff, and volunteers.

Monthly Giving Will Grow in Popularity

Monthly giving will grow in popularity for nonprofit organizations. A monthly giving program can be the best decision you can make to transform your nonprofit fundraising.

The benefits of a vibrant monthly giving program go beyond the revenue. Beyond increased annual giving, more predictable income, longer-term commitments, and increased annual giving, a monthly giving program also increases loyalty — and donor retention — and is easier for donors. These donors are also among your most loyal donors: 53.6% of COVID-19 donors are enrolled in a recurring giving program.[xxiii]

The most successful nonprofits focus their efforts. They find one tactic that works and then invest their efforts there. It may take trying five or six different things, but once you find a channel that earns a good income, focus your efforts to invest and grow that area until you can't grow it anymore.

Let me make the case about why monthly giving should be the area you invest in.

The first reason is donor value. The average recurring donor will give you 42% more in one year than donors who give single, separate gifts.

Donor acquisition is expensive. If you're able to generate 42% more income from a monthly donor than a single one-time donor, it helps pay off your donor acquisition quicker.

The increased donor value also increases your ability to do good work. What all could your programs team do if you delivered 42% more revenue to them this year?

Not only is the short-term donor value better, but the lifetime value is excellent. Recurring donors are worth 5.4 times more than one-time donors. If the lifetime giving of a one-time donor is $300, the lifetime value of a recurring donor is $1,620. When I was at Food for the Hungry, the lifetime value of a monthly donor was over $2,000!

Recurring donors are more likely to give beyond one year. According to Fundraising Effectiveness Project, recurring donors are more than twice as likely to give beyond one year when compared to single donors.

Our role as fundraising leaders is to build relationships with donors, so they view your nonprofit as an extension of their generosity. When donors give year after year, you're succeeding in this part of your job.

Another measure that demonstrates your success as a fundraising professional is that median revenue donors are giving. When you have a high median total revenue, you're building deep relationships with donors. The 2017 Target Analytics Survey found that median revenue for monthly giving is $320 per year, increasing from $305 in 2013. Monthly donors give a lot to your cause.

Donors enjoy giving. They enjoy giving because you're providing them a way to express their love for other people or a worthy cause. Giving $240 at one time is a challenge for many donors, but giving $20 per month is more manageable. By providing this flexibility, donors receive joy knowing their gifts will be used in a good way. It is convenient because they can set up giving just as they do for everything else — automatic, withdrawn each month.

For your nonprofit, monthly giving is a valuable way to create predictable income over a period of time. Monthly income provides predictable cash flow, so you aren't raising all your income in a few months. Many nonprofits raise most of their funds (many raise 50%) during the last quarter of the calendar year: October, November, December. Monthly giving income is consistent and predictable.

Donors feel joy when they give. They want to see that girl saved from sex trafficking, or that child receive an education, or a veteran receive job counseling, or a mom reunited with her kids. They receive joy when they know they're contributing. Monthly giving allows people to feel joy each month.

How do you create a successful monthly giving program?

Develop a donor persona. The donor persona is a crucial step in your monthly giving program development. The persona is an example of a monthly donor and describes very precisely who the person is. When you create the right persona and align your marketing and ongoing communications to this persona, your chance for donor retention and high long-term value for the donor increases.

In surveys, donors often tell us they want to feel like they belong to a community. They want to share the giving experience with other like-minded people. When you're developing your persona, begin thinking about ways you can connect similar donors. How can you build community?

A few years ago, amid a conversation about our ad spend, several team members debated the audience we were targeting with advertising. I commented about going after our donor persona, the donors who gave.

One of my staff said, "Well, maybe we have the wrong donors."

A few weeks later, she started calling this imaginary donor who didn't donate to our organization the "aspirational donor." The donor she wanted, not the ones we had.

Now, you may have a different donor in mind for a monthly giving program, and it makes sense to tailor your persona to the donor who is most likely to give. But be wise in who you're targeting and the data you have to support the conclusion that this is the right donor persona.

How do we figure out who our donor is? If you have an existing donor file, you can use surveys to identify answers to the questions to define the persona. You can also get a data append. For a data append, you provide a list of people to a data aggregator, and they provide back information you don't have. For example, with a list of donor names and contact information, you can often add in demographics such as income level, donor profiles, home valuation, employer, and shopping behaviors.

Finally, countless market research companies will tell you a great deal of information about your donors for a price.

Let's name your donor.

- What would you like to call him or her?
- How old is the donor?
- Describe your monthly donor in demographic terms:
  - education level
  - where the donor lives
  - whether the donor is religious
  - what kind of hobbies the donor enjoys
  - what kind of music the donor listens to
  - what TV channels or radio stations the donor tunes in to
  - details about the donor's family
- Where does the donor work?

- What is his or her profession?

Why does the donor support your cause? Why is it important to him or her? What pain point do you solve with this donation?

Brand your monthly giving program. An animal charity based in South Carolina started a monthly donor program without a name or brand, and it languished for months. After renaming the giving program to The Brigade and designing a unique look and feel for the monthly giving program, it took off, and now it has generated nearly $1 million in recurring revenue.

Why do you want to brand your monthly donor program?

First, it shows people they are a part of something unique. People like feeling special, and we consistently find in donor surveys that they want to be part of a community. Giving them something to rally around and know they are a part of will create happier donors.

Second, when you name your monthly donor with something that aligns with your brand, mission, and values, you further develop your primary brand. When you establish your primary brand, you're able to create more brand loyalty among your donors. We often think of donors as "our donors," when, in reality, you are one of many nonprofits your donor supports. Your donors' ultimate goal is to do something good and see a positive change in the world.

When you align your brand with those expectations, you have a greater chance of continuing to receive support.

Finally, when you name your monthly donor program, you give it credibility. People believe it's more official when it has a name — and are more likely to support it, even if just a little bit.

Project Concern uses the name "Think Forward" for its monthly giving program. This brand positioning helps donors think of the future as they join the program. This is an excellent example of helping position the donor for expectations of what is to come.

There's an element of caution here: ensure you name your program as an extension of your brand. You're not creating a new nonprofit; you're extending your nonprofit into monthly giving. For example, with charity: water, the monthly program called The Spring is a brand extension of charity: water and doesn't threaten the primary brand name.

Can you move forward without a name? Sure, we did it as Food for the Hungry because the product itself (child sponsorship) had a strong understanding in the market. We could simply say, "You're sponsoring a child," and people understood what we meant.

Acquire monthly donors. "Let's stay away from the name Hope Partners," one development director said. "A few years ago, we tried launching a monthly giving program and it failed miserably. This is our second attempt, and we don't want to relive the past."

Too often, monthly giving programs like "Hope Partners" at this particular nonprofit die off because of a lack of acquisition strategy. A lot of hard work goes into developing a recurring giving program that is brand-relevant and funds appealing work, but little thought is given to *how* to acquire donors. Many organizations believe creating a monthly giving program will result in existing donors flocking to it without realizing how difficult it is to actually acquire recurring donors.

Start acquiring donors from your single-gift donors and from people who are committed to your nonprofit organization, like volunteers. Next, explore other acquisition channels to acquire monthly donors, such as events, radio, direct mail, telemarketing, and digital.

If you are a nonprofit fundraising leader, one of the most critical parts of your job is to find new donors. Monthly giving programs have been proven to be one of the most effective forms of fundraising for nonprofits. Building recurring giving will be vital as a foundation for your organization's success in the post-pandemic world.

Even after a pandemic, fundraising fundamentals still apply. You must still build relationships with donors, demonstrate impact, and show gratitude. The pandemic has opened up new opportunities for nonprofits willing to think innovatively and develop or expand new giving programs. A key area your nonprofit should be developing is virtual fundraising. In the next chapter, we'll explore how nonprofit organizations are embracing these types of opportunities.

It's a Virtual World

Somo, an entrepreneurship accelerator nonprofit working in low-income urban areas of Kenya, provides training programs to help people start their own businesses. When the lockdowns began to spread, the organization digitized its training programs. The company also shifted *how* it trained people, adding gamification and new learning techniques to the virtual training program to increase its appeal among people who found themselves needing it most. The company also added new content for how to create sustainable businesses that survive even a country-wide lockdown.

This new channel required a faster Internet connection than most of the program participants have. The company began offering Internet data services to people and created content that worked even on basic-feature cell phones. With these changes, the organization expanded the people it served to a much broader audience in Kenya.

Organizations like Somo are adapting and innovating in this challenging environment. They adapt by creating virtual options for fundraising, staff interactions, and meeting the beneficiaries' needs.

Increased Virtual One-on-One Interaction

A friend who supports a couple organizations at a major donor level shared how the pandemic has changed his interactions with people from those organizations. "In the past, a 30-minute coffee meant much more than 30 minutes," John said. "I'd have to account for traffic in getting there and returning to my office. The interruption during the day would disrupt the flow of business for me. It's not easy for me to 'turn it off' and then 'turn it on' again during the workday. I care about these organizations, and a 30-minute Zoom call is much more reasonable and fits my day better."

Like many major donors, John's most valuable resource is time. He loves the causes of the organizations he supports and wants to meet with the representatives, but the demands on his time prevented most meetings. Now, John doesn't have to worry about traveling across town or canceling appointments at the last minute when his business needs him. "Even after COVID, I plan to keep using video calls because of the flexibility they offer," John added.

Like John, many of your donors enjoy the flexibility of group and one-on-one video calls. After the pandemic, keeping a video call in your tool set will help you accomplish more, reduce travel, and meet more donors using a channel they appreciate. There are a few keys to keep in mind for these calls:

What is the purpose of your call? First, you must determine why you're setting up a call with the donor. If you don't have a purpose, you won't be able to set a goal for what you want the donor to do.

There are four primary types of donor calls:

1. **Donor Cultivation:** This is the most common type of call when most of the relationship-building happens with a donor. There are no financial asks during cultivation calls.
2. **Thank You:** Whenever a donor takes action with a nonprofit, such as giving a gift or volunteering time, it's the perfect opportunity to call and say, "Thank you."
3. **Pre-Ask:** This uncommon call is handy if your organization is launching a fundraising campaign, but you're not ready to ask for money. You can call and determine the level of interest a donor may have in the campaign.
4. **Ask:** In this call, you'll ask the donor to take action — give a financial gift, volunteer, attend an event, or serve in some capacity.

Check in on your donor. The first question you should ask the donor is, "How are you doing during this time?" Even after the pandemic has passed, the donor's situation may still be challenging. Be authentic in how you talk with the donor. The relationship with any donor as a human being is first and foremost.

Learn more about your donor. Ask questions to learn more about your donor. You'll develop a deeper relationship and identify ways in the future they may want to partner with your organization.

Create layers of interaction with the donor. Unfortunately, there's high turnover for many organizations' donor development teams. Every major donor should have at least two people from an organization whom they know. For the highest capacity donors, this may be the CEO or Executive Director and the major donor representative. Other organizations may let the donor development team lead and the representative work with a donor. When there is turnover, it is much easier to transition the major donor to a new representative if there is one constant relationship.

Fundraising Events

At World Concern, we entered 2020 planning our annual 5k to end trafficking. The event, held Mother's Day weekend, typically drew in 2,500 participants, with hundreds more in attendance navigating the streets around our campus in Shoreline, Washington. As it became increasingly evident in the spring that Seattle and its surrounding area would implement stay-at-home orders, we decided to transition the in-person event to a virtual one.

We expanded the audience to include nationwide supporters and revised our fundraising goal down from $160,000 to $100,000. We asked participants to "run, walk, hike, or bike" the 5k in their own area in a safe and socially distanced manner. Instead of 2,500 registrants, we had a few hundred. We raised $90,000, almost hitting the revised goal.

Each September, World Concern hosts an annual in-person Transform Gala in Seattle for mid-level and major donors. The event features a formal dinner, live entertainment, and an opportunity to continue supporting

World Concern's work. 2020 forced us to reimagine the Gala. Fortunately, our donors rallied around the effort and contributed more than $600,000!

We learned valuable lessons with these two virtual fundraising events:

Get your board or major donors involved. The Transform Gala planning committee involved several board members and major donors. In previous years, this core group had several volunteer jobs, especially the night of the event. Moving the event virtually required different involvement from this team. This was an essential part of our planning process as we involved the committee in decisions such as:

What should the theme for the evening be? (Our theme was "From Seed to Garden.")

Should we charge for tickets to the event? (We decided not to.)

What should we send to registrants? (We sent a World Concern branded bag, two face masks, and seed bombs.)

Should we have food or wine? (We opted not to have a food option but to surprise key major donors and board members with wine.)

Should we offer registrations for "virtual tables" (small groups in homes) and individuals? (We offered individual registrations only and encouraged people to be safe if they planned on inviting others to experience the evening with them.)

Who should we ask to provide music for the evening? (We engaged Christian recording artist Danny Gokey to perform.)

These were just some of the decision points the committee helped with as we developed the virtual gala.

Another key benefit to creating a gala committee is that this group typically has influence and can be powerful representatives for inviting others to register for the event. Help your planning committee identify potential invitees and make the invitation.

Consider hiring a consultant. World Concern engaged with Premier Donor Strategies (https://premierdonorstrategies.com/) to help us develop the evening's strategy and produce the event. We were impressed with their experience producing live events and pivoting to digital events with clients during the pandemic. The decision to hire Premier was vital to the success we had that evening. Premier helped us form the run of show, gave us strategic advice for what to include, and, more importantly, what not to include. Premier also handled the production elements of the evening in their studio in Kansas City.

Develop a theme. The theme for the Transform Gala, "From Seed to Garden," gave us maximum flexibility as it represented both the opportunity to plan metaphoric seeds to help beneficiaries grow while also helping us provide actual seeds to help provide food to hungry people. We integrated the theme into everything from the invitations to the topics presented throughout the event.

Be prepared to look at every facet of the event. From the invitations to the thank-you notes, we looked at everything we did for past galas and considered how they would translate to the virtual environment.

For example, for an in-person gala, a winery would donate hundreds of bottles of wine for the event, and we would host a full sit-down dinner. For the virtual event, we received donated wine (which we delivered to a handful of significant donors and board members) and had to consider what to do about food (we decided not to offer a food option).

An in-person event doesn't translate directly to a virtual event. *This may be the most helpful advice in this section*: You don't (and shouldn't) take an in-person event and try to map the run-of-show to a virtual event directly. It doesn't work. An in-person event has the benefit of keeping people in the room for the entire evening. A virtual event can be closed in a second, and if you lose the viewer's interest it's challenging to get it back. Don't pivot too far, though — an effective virtual event is more than a Zoom call. A great virtual event:

- Has a runtime no longer than an hour.

- Quickly moves through each segment and into the next.
- Contains a variety of segments, e.g. pre-produced videos, interviews, music, audience Q&A with the participants, a peer testimonial, beneficiary impact stories, and appeals.
- Sticks to a firm run-of-show plan.

Get personal with your invitations. Your invitation strategy will determine a successful event. It's not enough to send out a save-the-date card, a paper invitation, and an email and expect sufficient attendance. Instead, get on the phones and call or text message invitees to get a firm commitment to register. Send them reminder emails leading up to the event. We sent a reminder the day before and the afternoon of the event. The donor relations team also followed up with invitees to make sure they remembered the event and attended.

Use a professional host. At Food for the Hungry, we sponsored and hosted hundreds of fundraising events. A key to conversion is hiring and training the right people to host the event. For the virtual Transform Gala, we hired Karyn Williams, a professional event host and musician who has done hundreds of events in the past decade (http://karynwilliams.com). As a professional, Ms. Williams understands the key elements that make up a good evening:

- Creating a personal connection with the audience
- Excellent storytelling

- Continuity from beginning to end
- A willingness to commit to the donation appeal and move people up giving levels
- A stage presence to lift other participants to great presentations

I've seen some organizations use a staff member or executive to host a virtual event, and, though it might work out, it doesn't have the *impact* of a professional.

Virtual events aren't limited to once a year. Hosting an in-person gala uses a considerable amount of time and monetary resources. Most nonprofits limit their events to one per year.

A virtual event is different. First, it costs much less than an in-person event. The World Concern Transform Gala cost one-third of the in-person gala and had a return on investment of over 10:1!

Second, virtual events require less manpower. Even with volunteers, it takes a lot of time to host an in-person event. A virtual event requires much fewer people to be successful.

Third, a virtual event can be created in a shorter period of time. A well-produced and attended virtual event can be created in four to six weeks. Most in-person galas take literal months to plan.

Finally, virtual events can take different forms. At World Concern, we're considering a spring fundraising event for a specific project or cause. Instead of a large general virtual gala, this one will be shorter and focused on one specific need. The flexibility of being virtual allows you to plan for more than one successful event a year.

What is the future for destination events? Do virtual options mean destination fundraising events are over?

A destination fundraising event is typically hosted at a vacation destination and is designed to draw in high-capacity donors to give a significant gift. To answer the above questions: no, destination events aren't over. It may take some time for high-capacity donors to want to participate in a destination fundraising event, but it remains an effective tool for major donor fundraising.

Virtual events may not completely replace in-person events; however, the emergence of effective virtual events adds another tool to our fundraising toolbelt.

Program Service Delivery

How you deliver services may not make sense during the pandemic and into the near future. Mothers2Mothers employed local women living with HIV in Africa as frontline health workers. As African countries began instituting lockdowns, the organization created the Virtual Mentor Mother Program to respond to the need for COVID-19 health support in countries with little to no healthcare infrastructure. The initiative engaged virtual health workers to help at the local level.

A secondary benefit is that the organization began collecting essential health data for local governments, mapped out hotspots for outbreaks, and delivered interventions where needed most.

Safeguarding your staff and beneficiaries may also require you to change how you deliver services in the post-pandemic world. Many experts predict we're on the cusp of more endemics and pandemics, and if this will in fact occur, nonprofit organizations will need to rethink how to deliver services to protect staff and beneficiaries safely.

Your organization may find it necessary to expand your charter. You may find it necessary to expand where and how you deliver your programs and services. As the lockdowns in the United States led to economic concerns for millions of families and the chance for many of those families to end up homeless, Georgia charity New Story developed a crowdfunding mechanism, PayTheirRent.org, to help 100 families pay their rent for three months. The organization's mission is to fight global homelessness, and this initiative helped expand its base of support to the U.S.

Your organization may be focused on a specific international cause, but the pandemic has forced you to pivot. You may find it necessary to expand the definition of who you support even after the pandemic is over.

Create focused teams to explore alternate program delivery. One large international NGO is working on a mobile app to help answer common questions and provide video-based training to volunteers in communities they work in. The community members can ask questions through their own language and get back video instruction. For example, a community member might ask, "How much should I water my garden?" and will receive video answers on how frequently to water the garden.

Your organization may find it necessary to explore new technology solutions for services previously delivered by human staff. This doesn't eliminate the need for staff but instead expands your capacity to take on new and challenging programs and services.

Create a cross-functional team to explore different ways to deliver your services and how the services must change to reflect the new reality. The key to this team is flexibility and an open mind for how your organization can best move forward and develop effective results.

Overcoming the digital divide. There are two distinct divides that we must overcome in the nonprofit sector for working remotely with beneficiaries.

First, we must overcome the digital access divide. Not all the people we serve have easy access to high-speed Internet or the skills necessary to navigate new technology platforms.

"Those who need our help most also require the most effort to reach. If we are serious as a sector about using technology to provide help in a nimble and adaptive way, we have to be intentional about how we account for language barriers, the digital divide, and other barriers to access," Justine Zinkin, of Neighborhood Trust, said.

The second challenge is that remote interactions do not allow for the creation of trust for some clients like in-person interactions do. Justine Zinkin explained, "Investment in user experience and back-end technology can allow an organization like ours to maintain human touch and personal relationships, even as our coaching happens over the phone or Zoom. However, tech-enabled services are not one-size-fits-all, nor does remote access inherently preserve a sense of connection and trust between provider and client."

Board and Leadership Meetings

Before the pandemic, many nonprofit boards preferred only in-person meetings. Many boards found virtual meetings to lack the interaction and body language necessary for effective communication. After boards held several virtual meetings in 2020, they have discovered an effectively designed virtual board meeting can in fact accomplish many of the goals of in-person meetings. It may not end in-person meetings altogether, but having a mix of virtual and in-person meetings can benefit the board and the organization.

There are several keys to holding virtual board meetings:

Do the pre-work. Encourage board members to read the board book before the meeting and get work accomplished beforehand. This may involve setting up committees to focus on a specific problem that can be presented to the board in a shorter period of time than a typical board presentation. If a board member doesn't come prepared, it can reduce the entire board's effectiveness.

Ask everyone to turn on cameras. Video conference fatigue is real, yet the benefits of seeing everyone outweigh the discomfort. Ask board members to keep video on and audio muted during the meetings. Having eye contact and seeing facial expressions helps bring the meeting alive for participants.

Shorten the sessions. PowerPoint presentations that last 45 minutes tire anyone in person and can be even worse virtually. Shortening presentations and allowing time for discussion will help focus your meeting on essential items.

Replicate networking times. Relationships often develop over dinner and social hours outside of typical board meetings. Without this time, it's vital to provide virtual networking options for board members to continue to develop these relationships. Try a virtual social event or replicate discussions by asking everyone to share one high and one low — professional or personal — during the board meeting.

Ensure you're following the law. Virtual board meetings require just as much care as in-person meetings, so ensure you're following the law by creating and passing minutes and keeping detailed records.

Bring in an expert. A virtual board meeting allows some creativity in agenda settings. Some organizations are using this as an opportunity to bring in experts from other industries to offer insights in 10- to 15-minute blocks. An expert can help grow the board's capacity or show how other organizations are innovating.

The pandemic forced nonprofit organizations to rethink their delivery of services and interaction with stakeholders. Will the need for these innovative solutions dissipate after the pandemic is over? No. The need for creative ways to reach people will continue to flourish. Nonprofits that embrace virtual technologies will thrive in the post-pandemic world.

Transparency

The public's trust in nonprofits has declined to the point that the January 2020 Edelman Trust Barometer survey found that only 50% of the public trusts nonprofits, a two-point decline from the previous year.

Compare this to for-profit corporations: The public rated their trust here at over 60%. People trust organizations whose mission is to create a better world less than corporations whose mission is to earn money.

The good news is, the work nonprofits have accomplished during the pandemic has increased the public's trust level to 56%, according to the May 2020 Edelman Trust Barometer survey.[xxiv]

For many donors, volunteers, and employees, transparency is the key to winning their support. These supporters want easy access to your financial data and an understanding of how you do your work. A transparent nonprofit shares this information in a way that is easy to absorb and act upon.

Clarity for Staff

During the pandemic, it is vital to share necessary information with staff. A friend of mine is the Development Manager at a human services organization in New York City. The organization began having financial difficulties during the pandemic, but the executive leadership opted not to tell the staff. Unfortunately, things got so bad that most of the team was laid off — despite prior assurances (the week before) that everything was fine, that they would weather the storm. Currently, the organization is completely shut down.

Too many nonprofit staff experienced something similar during the pandemic.

There must be some separation of information between nonprofit leadership and the organization's staff, but many nonprofits err on the side of not sharing *enough*. When you remain open with your employees, you'll find their trust in your leadership will increase — even if the information isn't positive news.

Sharing information goes beyond the financials. Employees are becoming more interested in understanding the organization's long-term plans and strategy. They want to know that the leadership team appreciates and trusts them. They want the ability to provide feedback and feel heard. Staff want to be more involved and know that their investment into a nonprofit is paying off.

In June, Oxfam shared its plans with staff for organizational changes before revealing a new strategic plan for the next decade. The organization is consulting with staff about the plan to save £16 million annually and expects this reorganization to result in the loss of more than 200 jobs. This comes on the heels of the organization's announcement that it is planning to cut 1,450 staff members and withdraw from 18 countries.

"The financial reality — not least the ongoing and uncertain impact of Covid — requires us to act now to ensure we live within our means. We will continue to consult fully and fairly with staff ... in reaching a final decision," said Danny Sriskandarajah, Oxfam GB Chief Executive.

Though Oxfam is going through a difficult organizational downsizing, the effort to involve staff in the strategic planning process will produce feelings of goodwill and foster trust. When you have an organizational crisis, do you involve staff in the process? Are there ways you can be more transparent with your team? When staff don't have clarity, they begin to worry. When staff members begin to worry, they start looking for new jobs. Don't lose your team from a lack of clarity.

Freely share information with staff. While, again, there must be some separation of information between leadership and workers, more nonprofits need to remain open with their employees.

We faced many unknowns as the pandemic started, and that hasn't changed. As leaders, we're challenged by an unknown future. During this time, CRISTA's leadership team was open and honest about our financial situation and the steps we were taking to ensure the organization survived. It hasn't been easy, but we've kept our staff informed along the way. Clear and honest communication is vital for employees to trust the organization.

Donors Will Demand Increased Transparency

Donors have so many options and increasingly will exercise the opportunity to stop giving to an organization they don't perceive as communicating transparently.

Share openly and often. You may believe your nonprofit is being transparent by posting audited financial statements and 990s, but the truth is: you're not doing enough. Nonprofits committed to being transparent and honest have a higher chance of building strong relationships with donors.

Donors crave transparency from nonprofits.

In the United States, nonprofit organizations are required by law to provide a certain level of financial transparency. They are required to disclose certain financial information upon request. However, organizations should go above and beyond the legally required standard to attract and gain their new supporters' trust.

Elevating your level of transparency encourages people to trust your organization.

A transparent organization is willing to frequently and openly share results. Your organization should always share information and post it on an easy-to-find page on your website. Food for the Hungry's financial page is consistently one of the top five most-visited pages on our site. People want more information about your organization — so give it to them!

PSI, a health services nonprofit, creates a monthly impact report. This open access to its impact data and its performance helps keep supporters informed about what PSI is doing. The monthly impact report helps donors learn more about the organization's work and how it uses the donation. Donors love knowing exactly where their money will go and how it's impacting real lives.

Make your information easy to find. Post your financial information, such as IRS form 990, audited financial statements, and annual reports, on your website.

Certain nonprofits make it challenging to access this type of financial detail. For example, some large organizations require people to request their financial information or 990 forms in writing. Unnecessary barriers like these discourage people from supporting organizations because it makes them look less transparent.

In addition, list your board members and executive team on your website. When someone is interested in your organization, they'll research your website for more information. Providing the names of your board members and executive team with good bios helps people develop more confidence in your charity.

Funders Desire Clear Plans and Projections

One funder I work with requires nonprofits she invests in to develop a three-year strategy. In her experience, an organization that can provide a detailed three-year plan has a better chance of succeeding with her funding. Her ultimate goal isn't to help a nonprofit accomplish a specific short-term program but to see the nonprofit grow and thrive after the funding is complete.

To that end, she invests a considerable amount of time and resources to helping the nonprofit understand revenue and create sustainable income. Funders of the future don't want to see just one project accomplished, they desire the nonprofit to create positive, long-term transformation from their funding.

Being transparent also has an impact on foundation and institutional fundraising. For example, a South Boston church-based youth club offers a nursery, playgroups, computer and music classes, and other services to children regardless of their religion. A family foundation in Boston whose mission is to improve the quality of life of the deprived, disadvantaged, and excluded was hesitant to fund the youth club without seeing a reliable track record and impact reporting. Though the foundation didn't usually accept unsolicited grant applications, they were willing to work with the priest who managed the youth club to explain how to attract funding.

The foundation suggested the youth club perform an independent organizational assessment to:

- Understand the organizational effectiveness in a broader context of what services South Boston needs and what organization can meet those needs.

- Provide insight into the many activities already in place in the church and identify the need for more.

- Uncover the vision for the future of the youth club.

The organizational assessment led to a three-year relationship with the foundation. With a grant, the youth club could hire paid staff and expand its footprint in the community.

At smaller organizations, it can be challenging to expend the resources to go "above and beyond" for transparency. As this local youth club illustrates, being transparent can lead to great opportunities and growth for your nonprofit.

Nonprofit organizations face many funding challenges and need to become more transparent to ensure continued, strong relationships with employees, donors, and large funders.

Artificial Intelligence

Benefits Data Trust developed an AI-powered machine learning model to help call center employees assist new registrants for SNAP Benefits. The system helps identify the level of assistance an enrollee may require. It monitors the application and document submission process and identifies cases that may require a hands-on approach.

The nonprofit's CEO implemented the system to help it become more efficient and provide better service to beneficiaries.

Artificial Intelligence tools like the one Benefits Data Trust developed can help organizations improve donor service, help more people, enhance the donor experience, and automate previously manual processes.

Savvy nonprofits are deploying these tools to help them leverage resources. After the pandemic, your organization should review how it can implement AI tools to improve operations.

Personalize the Donor Experience

Artificial Intelligence tools are helping nonprofits change fundraising, which is in the midst of a vibrant new landscape. As donation rates continue to decline, many organizations seek new ways to engage donors to raise funds. Personalized donor experience is one way fundraisers can help their organizations thrive.

For example, by investing in AI, nonprofits can use data analysis techniques like machine learning and natural language processing to make personalized messages for each donor who enters into giving conversations with them via social media or email.

In addition to improving the donor experience, this tactic also allows fundraisers to spend more time engaging with donors since AI suggests daily interactions while still delivering relevant content that resonates with each person's interests.

Though AI has been around for decades, recent computational power advancements make it much more affordable for nonprofit organizations of all sizes. Nonprofits can now use powerful tools to improve fundraising and develop relationships with donors.

AI tools for fundraising include:

Online chatbots. Chatbots are becoming more and more popular because they offer a convenient way for supporters to get a quick answer to their questions. Maintaining customer service is difficult when dealing with large numbers of supporters. Still, chatbot technology can alleviate this challenge by making it easier than ever to provide individualized support. Chatbots also help reduce wait times on phone lines and other communication methods like email or social media channels. This allows nonprofit organizations not only an opportunity to present themselves but also to maintain their professional tone throughout all contact methods. The level of service your organization provides donors can be a differentiator.

Identifying potential donors. Artificial Intelligence is being used to help identify potential nonprofit donors in your database. AI tools are excellent at recognizing similarities between people profiles. Tools can help find new potential donors by analyzing the demographic profile of current donors, their giving history, and their likes and interests. These software tools can also suggest what to appeal for, the giving matrix you should use for various donors, and an appeal's timing.

Personalizing appeals. The right algorithms can help you analyze donor data and personalize your fundraising appeals. Software tools perform an analysis of a donor's data and giving patterns suggesting to the charity what kind of message will be most effective.

Provide Improved Services to Beneficiaries

Innovative nonprofits are developing AI-based tools to help beneficiaries. Crisis Text Line uses natural language processing to connect a suicide-intended person with the right counselor and help new counselors learn from more experienced counselors. By analyzing one million anonymized texts from nearly 3,500 counselors, Cornell researchers help the organization identify trends in how the counselors speak to help beneficiaries.

Hand Talk in Brazil built a Portuguese-to-Brazilian Sign Language digital avatar to enable digital communications for deaf Brazilians. The app translates voice and text automatically, providing a communications tool that has transformed users' lives.

In another example, Quill.org uses deep learning to provide low-income students immediate feedback on their writing, allowing them to improve their skills quickly. The organization's tools support over one million students, creating personalized learning plans based on the student's progress.

"There are 27 million low-income students in the United States who struggle with basic writing and find themselves disadvantaged in school and in the workforce," says Peter Gault, Quill.org's Executive Director. "And teachers struggle to help them, too. By using natural language processing to provide students with immediate feedback on their writing, we can help teachers support millions of students on the path to becoming stronger writers, critical thinkers, and active members of our democracy."

Nonprofits can also use AI to promote the wellness of their beneficiaries. From the nonprofit benefits carrier Green Shield Canada, Erin Crump recounted to the Charity Village website how the organization turned to AI tools when it became evident that diabetes was becoming a high-cost disease. They used analytics to identify the variables that predicted whether someone was likely to develop complex diabetes. Once they had that data, they created tools for beneficiaries to improve their health and wellness, thereby changing the disease's trajectory as early as possible.

Low-cost computing power and inexpensive AI tools have empowered nonprofits to create innovative solutions to help beneficiaries in new and exciting ways. The pandemic has forced many nonprofits to explore how they can offer services with fewer person-to-person interactions, and these circumstances will result in new solutions to impact far more lives than previously possible.

Improve Staff Access to Data and Analysis

Data analysis tools that use machine learning to present data and recommendations can help nonprofits and their staff do more nimble decision-making throughout the organization.

Tal Frankfurt, Founder of Cloud for Good, says AI is best used to:

- Automate processes
- Provide cognitive insights from data analysis
- Engage with people

Frankfurt says AI "does not get exhausted from running millions of scenarios or [being] interrupted by meetings."

Automate business processes. AI can help nonprofits on multiple levels, particularly in enhancing organizational operations. For example, AI-based tools can automate routine administrative tasks and help nonprofits improve fundraising, finances, communications, and human resources operations. Many AI tools can facilitate pre-hire screening based on the hiring manager's criteria regarding experience and skill sets desired.

As an added benefit, analysis software reviews the resumés of potential candidates without considering gender, age, race, or ethnicity, which eliminates biases that could steer the focus away from promising candidates. It also flags missing information from the resumés that the employer is looking for. Some AI tools can provide information about potential candidates not currently in the job market but who may seek employment in the future, all of which make the process of finding hires with the best fit more efficient.

The Brookings Institute TechTank blog notes: "In conjunction with machine learning and data analytics, it is a way to control costs, handle internal operations, and automate routine tasks within the organization. Adoption of these tools can help groups with limited resources streamline internal operations and external communications and thereby improve the way they function."

Other tasks that AI tools can handle for nonprofits include running reports, doing background research, and coming up with purposeful messages and timely calls to action. Using AI to automate some clerical tasks not only gives staff more time to devote elsewhere, such as interacting with beneficiaries or donors, it will also likely save the organization money in both the short- and long-term.

Analyze large amounts of data. Where AI tools do the heavy lifting is with data. What separates machine learning from human learning is its ability to analyze significant amounts of data. Every time we go online, whenever we buy something, with every government report, we spawn tons of data tied to banks, retailers, and industries. This blast of big data is so huge it is humanly impossible for our individual or collective brains to make practical sense of it. AI-driven analysis can identify observable patterns and predict likelihoods and trends, including donation projections, likely donors, and organizational finance operations.

A critical function of nonprofits is raising essential fundraising dollars. As a rule, the top 10% of the donor pool comprise 90% of donations, and a lack of resources makes it hard for many nonprofits to reach all the key donors who are potentially willing to make major donations. AI bots can rapidly break down donor datasets to locate the top contributors. AI can also analyze big data related to patterns of previous donations, amounts, and attendance at benefits. Nonprofits can then use that analysis to develop better engagement strategies like creating and sending personalized communications based on donor behavior, encouraging donors to contribute. Such tailored communication can double or triple daily outreach, resulting in better leads that should increase donations to the organization. The goal is not for nonprofits to use AI to replace fundraisers; it's to make fundraisers more successful and engaged.

It's a win-win: the nonprofit fosters more substantial relationships with its constituents while disclosing opportunities to generate more revenue. It's also an example of how AI tools can analyze and interpret data that would otherwise go unused and turn it into useful information to increase donations and protect finances.

Darrell West, Founding Director of the Center for Technology Innovation, and Theron Kelso, a Senior Consultant at Wipfli, said in *BizTech* magazine: "Fraud and corruption are major challenges for any kind of organization as it is hard to monitor every financial transaction and business contract. AI tools can help managers automatically detect actions that warrant additional investigation." They added that nonprofits could use AI to create early warning systems to spot abnormalities, identify unusual transactions, and minimize financial misconduct.

According to Forbes Council member Kevin Xu, even smaller nonprofits can utilize AI to handle finance and improve operations, sustainability, human resources, and communications. "Introducing AI seems like a daunting and costly challenge for most nonprofits, but it doesn't need to be. Once you evaluate your mission, simulate situations, and define goals, your nonprofit will be able to enjoy the benefits AI has brought to the private sector."

The best way to use AI isn't to get an algorithm and cross your fingers. As with any technology, it's only as good as how you use it. It's incumbent on nonprofits to identify their greatest needs, areas that could be automated, problems to solve, and the data to analyze that will result in a high return on investment to reach your goals.

Where Do We Go from Here?

The pandemic presented uniquely complex challenges to nonprofits, but not all the challenges were caused by the pandemic. Unfortunately, the nonprofit sector isn't finished with challenging times. Nonprofits will face various trials, including dealing with a possible economic downturn, increasing competition for funds and resources, or changing public attitudes toward philanthropy. The following several years will continue to present stress to nonprofit organizations.

The good news is that many positive trends are happening within the nonprofit community that will help us get through this difficult time. Nonprofit leaders must learn how to balance being proactive with being reactive — to look ahead and anticipate threats instead of attempting to change course after the fact.

The first trend your nonprofit must embrace in a post-pandemic world is to solidify your foundation by renewing your roots. Key questions you should ask:

1. Is your mission clear?
2. Are you focused on accomplishing your mission?
3. Are your staff, donors, and beneficiaries aligned with your mission?

The pandemic has tested the strength of many organizations' foundations. Keep focused on accomplishing your nonprofit's mission.

Next, the post-pandemic nonprofit should review and update — or create — a strategy. The strategy answers the question, "Is our organization doing the right things?" You will accomplish the strategic review by examining your strategic initiatives to ensure your organization is on-target and that the targets still make sense. Ensure that your leadership team, board of directors, and staff understand the strategy and their initiatives are aligned.

As a follow-up to the strategic review, focus on the performance of your programs. Ensure your programs and services are the most effective to ensure continued funding support. It may be time to change or eliminate underperforming programs.

About a quarter of nonprofit organizations have an enterprise risk management process. A key lesson the pandemic taught nonprofits is how essential risk management is to good organizational governance. Running a nonprofit without a risk management plan is a recipe for disaster. After the pandemic, creating or updating a risk management plan should be a priority.

Innovation is one of the most undervalued aspects of organizations. They are often driven to innovate with a lack of resources and funding. Without enough people to get something accomplished, nonprofits develop innovative solutions. This was especially true during the pandemic and will be a crucial part of managing a successful nonprofit organization after COVID-19. How does your nonprofit organization build an innovative culture?

1. Identify your organization's core competencies. What are you good at? How did you achieve excellence in those things?
2. Examine the fundamental assumptions about your work. What are you doing? How are you doing it? Where are you working? Why are you doing it this way?
3. Discuss your solutions with the people working directly with clients or beneficiaries.

Remote working has revolutionized the nonprofit workplace. Some 83% of office employees desire to continue working from home at least one day per week. As a nonprofit leader, you're faced with the challenge of designing the post-pandemic workplace for your organization. Your organization will need to compete for the best staffers as the for-profit sector is embracing remote working.

Another challenge facing nonprofits is how to keep staff, volunteers, and beneficiaries safe. Though we now have a vaccine, COVID-19 may never altogether leave us. Combined with the continued risk of new viruses, nonprofit organizations need to safeguard interactions.

The flexible nonprofit survives. The pandemic demonstrated to many organizations the need for more nimble programs. Creating scalable programs requires skillful leaders, flexible funding, and agile program design. As your nonprofit organization looks to create more agile programs, it may be time to explore how you distribute the programs. A key to this process to maintaining program quality. Your organization may choose to reinvent or adapt your programs to continue delivering effective results.

The pandemic has severely hampered movement of people and goods. The better that nonprofits prepare for logistical and travel restrictions caused by COVID-19 today, the better they will handle similar, future disasters. These restrictions are expected to continue for some time and may impact workers from getting work visas. This may force some nonprofits to hire more local staff for programs. One option that may be attractive for international NGOs is to increase the use of local partners.

Many organizations were surprised by giving in 2020. Despite the pandemic, people opened their wallets to support organizations they care about. There are no guarantees for the future, and many economists predict that governmental economic interventions will end, and the nonprofit sector will face several years of economic slowdown.

We did see a combination of a rejuvenation of direct mail and increased digital giving in 2020. Organizations that invested in robust multi-channel giving saw the benefits during the pandemic. People will continue supporting organizations through a variety of channels.

Cause-oriented giving will reduce donor loyalty to specific organizations. The next generation of donors is far less loyal to particular organizations and instead enjoys giving to a specific cause. Your nonprofit organization will need to create trust with donors to retain them.

Monthly giving will continue to grow as people change their giving habits to match how they transact in other areas of life. Your nonprofit should invest in a robust recurring giving program.

Not only has digital giving increased, but nonprofits were forced to digitize programs to continue serving people in 2020. Many of these virtual services will increase in the future as people become more comfortable with the technology and as organizations innovate ways to reach more people at a lower cost.

The need for nonprofit transparency has never been more evident. People want to trust that their donations will be used effectively. A transparent nonprofit shares this information in a way that is easy to absorb and act on.

Transparency isn't limited to donors. Your staff members want more information and decide how much they trust leadership by how much you're willing to share. When you remain open with your employees, you'll find their trust in your leadership will swell — even if the information isn't good news.

Artificial Intelligence has matured to a level that ensures every nonprofit can have access to tools to improve efficiency and capabilities. AI is being used to personalize the donor's experience, improve beneficiary services, automate the employee recruiting process, and analyze mountains of data.

Since the beginning of 2020, we've had to grow and adapt to a surreal situation and meet unexpected challenges. Through it, we've grown as leaders, and our organizations have become nimbler. As your organization navigates the years to come in a post-pandemic world, embracing these 12 trends will help you not only survive but thrive.

End Notes

i   https://www.washingtonpost.com/local/non-profits-coronavirus-fail/2020/08/02/ef486414-d371-11ea-9038-af089b63ac21_story.html

ii   http://gd7xi2tioeh408c7034706rc-wpengine.netdna-ssl.com/wp-content/uploads/2020/04/COVID-19-Nonprofit-Decision-Framework.pdf

iii   https://www.councilofnonprofits.org/tools-resources/operating-reserves-nonprofits

iv   https://worldwaterreserve.com/water-crisis/clean-water-charity-organizations/

v   https://ssir.org/articles/entry/nonprofit_mergers_that_work

vi   https://www.aicpa.org/press/pressreleases/2018/survey-organizations-do-not-have-enterprise-wide-risk-management.html

vii   https://grantcraft.org/content/blog/what-weve-learned-after-five-years-of-risk-management-in-philanthropy/

viii   https://www.pwc.com/us/en/library/covid-19/us-remote-work-survey.html

ix   https://www.forbes.com/sites/chrisstrub/2020/06/11/remotework/?sh=65f1edbc4224

x   https://www.cdc.gov/coronavirus/2019-ncov/community/guidance-business-response.html?CDC_AA_refVal=https%3A%2F%2Fwww.cdc.gov%2Fcoronavirus%2F2019-ncov%2Fspecific-groups%2Fguidance-business-response.html

xi   https://www.cdc.gov/coronavirus/2019-ncov/community/guidance-business-response.html?CDC_AA_refVal=https%3A%2F%2Fwww.cdc.gov%2Fcoronavirus%2F2019-ncov%2Fspecific-groups%2Fguidance-business-response.html

xii   https://www.nptechforgood.com/2020/06/06/10-must-know-stats-about-covid-19-donors/

xiii   https://solutions.volunteermatch.org/hubfs/Ebooks/The%20Impact%20of%20COVID-19%20on%20Volunteering%20-%20A%20Two%20Month%20Comparison.pdf

xiv   https://www.wallacefoundation.org/knowledge-center/Documents/Strategies-to-Scale-Up-Social-Programs.pdf

xv   https://www.cafamerica.org/covid19report/

xvi   ITC Charts Businesses' Path Through COVID-19 Crisis | News | SDG Knowledge Hub | IISD

xvii   Going Local 2.0: How to Reform Development Agencies to Make Localized Aid More Than Talk (ssir.org)

xviii   UNICEF-Oct-2019-Working-Paper-on-localization-.pdf (ifrc.org)

xix   https://lapafundraising.com/3707-2/

xx   https://www.compu-mail.com/statistics/direct-marketing-statistics-for-nonprofit-fundraisers xxi https://www.nptechforgood.com/2020/06/06/10-must-know-stats-about-covid-19-donors/

xxii https://www.multichannelnonprofit.com

xxiii https://www.nptechforgood.com/2020/06/06/10-must-know-stats-about-covid-19-donors/

xxiv https://www.edelman.com/sites/g/files/aatuss191/files/2020-05/2020%20Edelman%20Trust%20Barometer%20Spring%20Update.pdf

REVOLUTIONIZE YOUR NONPROFIT

LEARN HOW TO ATTRACT AND RETAIN DONORS, VOLUNTEERS, AND STAFF WITH *MAGNETIC NONPROFIT*

ARE YOU LOOKING FOR A WAY TO FIND AND RETAIN MORE DONORS? DO YOU WANT TO INCREASE YOUR NONPROFIT'S INCOME WHILE BUILDING LIFELONG DONORS? MAGNETIC NONPROFIT UNLOCKS THE SECRETS TO DONOR AND INCOME GROWTH.

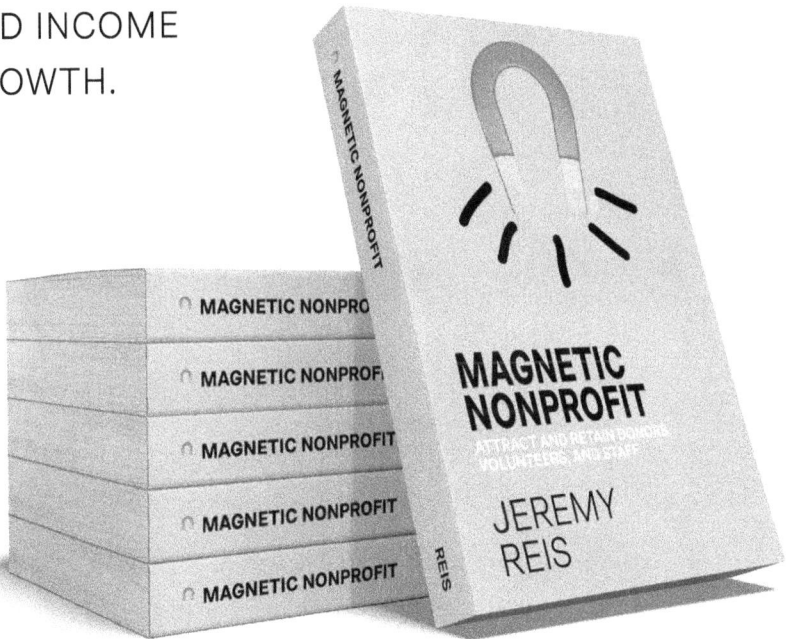

ORDER AT MAGNETICNONPROFIT.COM OR YOUR FAVORITE BOOKSELLER